TO: CYNTHIA,

LABELED:

ISBN 978-1-7340121-0-1
ISBN 978-1-7340121-2-5 (eBook)

Labeled: Ward of the State

Edited by Monique D. Mensah
Jacket design by Ana Grigoriu-Voicu
Interior design by Elena Jarmoskaite
Author photograph by Joyanne Panton

This is a work of creative non-fiction. The events are
portrayed to the memory of Kenisha. While all the stories
are true, some names and identifying details have been
changed to protect the privacy of the individuals involved.
The goal in all cases was to protect people's privacy without
damaging the integrity of the story.

For permission, questions and comments about the quality
of this book, please contact us at hello@kenishaanthony.com

www.kenishaanthony.com

KENISHA E. ANTHONY

a memoir

~~LABELED:~~

Ward of the state

WARD OF THE STATE – def; a person, usually a minor, who has a guardian appointed by the U.S dependency court system to care for and take responsibility for that person.

*This book is dedicated to children all over the world.
If you have yet to know it, I'll be the first to say, you can do
anything you set your mind to.*

Believe it. Do it!

CONTENTS

FROM THE AUTHOR

There was a moment when I had grown tired of talking about being an adult that was once in foster care. I wanted to move on with my life. I was established, employed, and had a home, clothes, and a car. I was doing well for myself. I felt I had overcome every practical challenge there was to being a foster kid, but my growth was overlooked once I shared my story. People continuously looked at me as a charity case, offering me things I didn't need such as worn clothes. It was like the label of being a helpless and needy kid had followed me. I vowed that if I have children, they will never have to tolerate the things I did. I'm not that kid anymore. I have something else to look forward to.

Although I was tired, life had a funny way of reminding me that it is important for me to share my story. One day, I received an e-mail. It was a message from a child client stating that he'd googled my name and learned I had been in foster care. He also sent me a friend request on Facebook. Considering what I had learned in training about employee/client boundaries, I was unsure of how to proceed. I knew him well enough; he was a good kid and his case plan goal was APPLA (short for "another planned permanent living arrangement"). I did not agree this was the most appropriate goal for his case. I recommended adoption as a better permanency plan. In his favor, there were people interested in becoming his forever family. However, he chose to age out of foster care after being persuaded by his first clinical therapist that a time-limited stipend was better than having long-term relationships. The money was more appealing to him, so my plea to him to weigh his options carefully didn't stand a chance. I respected his decision. To make sure his needs were met, I had done most of everything myself: appointments, school visits, etc. My supervisor teased me because of it. I just had to be sure things were done. Even still, I hesitated. I was puzzled by the fact he googled me. What prompted him to do that? I spoke with my supervisor and his therapist about the situation. They both gave me the okay to respond about my experience.

Putting myself in his shoes at seventeen, I answered his questions with enough information to ease his anxiety about aging out, without giving him an in-depth version of my life. One thing I always feared was what happened to my kids when they were no longer with me. I can't control that.

I know kids need to hear stories from those like themselves. They need hope that things can be okay. It was selfish for me to have thought to keep my story a secret, knowing there are other children in this world scared of the unknown just as I was.

I pondered how I was going to tell my story and make a lasting impact. I knew I wanted to write a book but had yet to find my niche. I thought, *The world doesn't want to hear another struggle story; who am I?* That was my insecurities speaking again. But as I listened to an episode of The Breakfast Club, Lena Waithe had a message during her interview. She said, "Being free is being able to make art that has not been touched by someone who hasn't walked in your shoes, embracing your gift, writing something meaningful to you. Be more than a writer. Be an activist. The world needs more representation of what's missing."

Michelle Obama's elegant presence as a strong black woman and the delivery of her powerful speech during the 2015 Black Girls Rock event inspired me. Through the television, I felt her speaking directly to me. I'd see her and say, "That's the kind of woman I want to be—black, strong, and impactful." In her memoir, *Becoming*, she preaches, "Share your story. The world needs to hear it!" During her show in Miami on her book tour, she must've said it more than a thousand times. Even though she couldn't hear me, every time she said it, I said, "I promise to finish this book. It's going to be a special piece of art."

I am becoming—stronger, wiser, and me.

No one ever said it would be easy. I can recall times when I was uncertain and ready to quit. My memoir is intended to share my process of living through disappointment, doubt, and confusion; seeking understanding; and, ultimately, finding my purpose on this earth. We all have something to contribute. I hope this social awareness tool will be a muse for how you view yourself, others, and the world.

Namaste,

Kenisha

INTRODUCTION

Bill of Rights

"Life is only about the I-Tried-To-Do."
- **Nikki Giovanni**

"On any given day, nearly 443,000 children are placed in the foster care system in the United States."
- **National Foster Youth Institute** (NFYI)

The life of a child labeled a Ward of the State is like a game of poker. Her life is at stake, so let's hope she has the luck of the Irish and is dealt a royal flush. Her welfare is solely dependent upon the ideas and actions of others: Chapter 39 of the Florida Statutes, administrative codes, human services professionals, family members, and others who may decide to help the situation.

How does this work? How will this end? Where will I live? Will my parents change their behavior? What services does my family need? Will the right recommendations be made on our behalf? Will my siblings and I stay together? If not, can I visit them? Will I meet them if they're not born yet? How long will this process take? Will quality services be provided for my family? If custody is released to a family member or someone else, will they have the financial means to care for me? Will they want to care for me? Will my family achieve reunification? Will my parents lose their parental rights? Am I going to be adopted? Do I need another planned permanent living arrangement? Is this permanency plan really permanent? Am I eligible to receive independent living services? If not, is there anything you can offer me? Does my case manager care?

These questions are all familiar to individuals who are subjected to the child welfare system in this country. As families maneuver through stages of the dependency process, the answers to these questions should be revealed as they apply to their specific case. However, some topics may not be applicable depending on circumstances. In my case, these topics were all relevant. I wanted the answers and had the right to know per Florida Statute 39.202(7)[1]. I do not recall having a conversation with any of my assigned case managers about the process to obtain the answers, which would have been in my foster care records. I'm pretty sure it never occurred. But, over time, I became curious and needed a clear understanding about what happened to my family so I could begin the healing process. I needed to understand the root cause of my pain and everyone's role in it. I needed to know if my parents at least tried. I turned to the system to gain an understanding of my childhood because it was like a lost treasure. I knew it existed, but it couldn't be found. I didn't have any pictures or videos of the younger me to jog my memory. There were only bits and pieces of information that didn't tell me much of anything.

Without knowledge, at age nineteen, I took action. I went to the children's courthouse to get detailed information about my life. Respectfully, I followed the records request process and awaited a response from the receptionist. Her reply was unusual. She said there was nothing in my file. I didn't understand what she meant. There was indeed a file, but it was empty? I asked her to give me the file with whatever little information it contained, and we entered a heated conversation because she refused and continued to say there was nothing in it.

I said, "There has to be something there, because I had a tuition exemption," which was a signed legal document that should've been in my file. Her tone and body language said it all; she was aggravated by my persistence. Without any knowledge of my rights, my attempt resulted in

---

1   **s. 39.202(7)(a)** — the department shall make and keep reports and records of all cases pertaining to a child and family until the child who is the subject of the record is 30 years of age and may then destroy the records. (a) Within 90 days after the child leaves the department's custody, the department shall give a notice to the young adult who was in the department's custody, which specifies how the records may be obtained.

an epic failure. I didn't get the file, but at least I had tried. I was okay with that, even though I was still at square one. I was left with one option—accept it and move on without the possibility of knowing the truth about what happened to my family. What I knew was what I had, and what I didn't know would just remain unknown.

Eight years later, at age twenty-seven, I tried again, this time, with more knowledge than before. My mentor, Geori Berman, had enlightened me about my right to view my own file. She also took the extra step of telling me exactly who I needed to contact and what detailed information should be included in the records request. There I was again, trying to put the pieces to the puzzle together. I sent an e-mail to the contact Geori had given me, only to receive an awkward reply explaining that he no longer worked for the agency.

I was confused. How had he responded to his work email if his last day with the agency was during the prior week? Why did he still have access to his e-mails? Every process with the system was a runaround. His e-mail did not include information about the new person taking on the role. So I forwarded the e-mail to Geori, and she reached out to her resources for accurate information. A few days later, she provided two other persons of contact for me to send the request to.

A month passed, and I still hadn't heard anything. I sent a follow-up e-mail, and a representative responded, assuring me they were working diligently to produce the file. I thought there must be a lot of information for it to take so long, which contradicted the "There's nothing there" chant I'd gotten during the first attempt to get my records.

Another month had gone by when I finally received a notification—an e-mail including an encrypted file. My heart started pounding, and I had to pause, asking myself if I wanted the answers I had longed for. A part of me wanted to delete it, but I didn't.ᵂ I took a deep breath and proceeded to enter the security codes to access the file and learn about my life.

While reading through all 861 pages, I had to catch my breath several times. The monsoon of emotions became too much for me at times. I didn't want to believe I was reading about my own family and self. I shed tears along the way. A few times, I walked away, feeling like I didn't want to know any more. Other parts of me were angry.

I wanted to question people about things they'd said about me, but I couldn't, because I didn't know exactly who had said what. It was documented that I was a liar, had made things up in my head, and should be referred for a psychological evaluation. This was the underlying reason I never talked to people about what was happening or what I was feeling or going through. People always claimed something was mentally wrong with me. To be fair, there was; I was a confused child yearning for love from my absent parents. I didn't know where to channel those emotions. And, in the midst of battling the hardships of their absence, I was being mistreated. No one came around to being honest with themselves or me about the hurtful things they'd done to me.

Once I finished reading the file, I had more questions for the system. The document was not in chronological order. I found an investigation summary report from 1996 tucked away in the middle of the file, detailing allegations made against my mother, Regina Walker, AKA Gina. The report stated:

Over the past 4 months, the mother has been using her 1900-dollar social security check on drugs rather than on the needs of the children. The mother has been told a number of times to provide clothing for the children and she refused to do so. The older 2 children do not have anything to wear to school. The 4-year-old only has a few old clothes that relatives have given to her. The mother was evicted 2 weeks ago and has had no contact with her children since that time.

The outcome of the investigation and actions taken by the courts were also included. The children were released to a relative with court-ordered services, including supervision—services that my older sister, Ashley, claimed she didn't recall my family participating in. The file included a few home visit notes and an indication of recommended services and agencies that were supposed to have provided therapeutic treatment for us, but there were no attached case plans, judicial reviews, service referrals, court orders, case notes, or status reports to support the ruling.

After 1997, there were no further indications that the case against Gina had continued, so I don't know how the case proceeded or how it closed. In 2008, another case was called in to the child abuse hotline. A case was initiated and concluded with verified findings of inadequate supervision and abandonment and failure to provide living arrangements, supervision, and other needs. I saw an unusual notation that stated it was unknown if I had spent time in licensed care. What did that mean?

Several records contained discrepancies as to whether my mother and father's parental rights had been terminated (TPR'd).[2] There was an adoption home-study to assess the home and life of a prospective adoptive parent before allowing an adoption to take place, but there was no clear indication of approval or denial. From my understanding of the child welfare system, adoption wouldn't have been pursued unless my parents had been TPR'd or were soon to be.

I was shocked to see something about a step-dad referenced in the file. I've never had or lived with a step-dad. The only step-dad I could've had was my mom's husband who had passed away before I was born. Maybe it was a simple mistake. It was documented that my maternal aunt, Shawn, had been my legal guardian since 1996. She had been granted shared custody, although my primary placement was with my grandmother, Rose. I'd only lived with Shawn for about three years of my life. After I moved out, she claimed to have legally relinquished all custodial rights for me. I don't know how Shawn claimed to have done it without going before a judge, or which state employee failed to document it. Other information was wrong and hard to understand due to terrible handwriting and redactions.

Over the years, more incidents occurred involving the Department. The Department had been well aware that I was no longer in the care of my alleged legal guardian, Shawn, and neither of us wished to be reconnected. But new investigations continued to be closed with no indicators, which meant

---

2   **TPR** — the termination of a mother or father as the legal parent of a child.

that either the investigator didn't have any concerns or found no evidence to confirm the allegations that started the case, landing me in the care of individuals who didn't have legal rights to care for me.

The file was not helpful at all, as pieces of my life remain unknown. It only proved that the pitfalls of the child welfare system can be damaging to the lives of those who encounter it. I wondered if the system gave my family a fair chance to engage in treatment to achieve reunification.

Through research, I learned that during that era, the Department was under a lot of scrutiny and transition. The foster care system was battling several lawsuits. Children were missing, case workers were overworked, quitting, and falsifying legal documents to get by. I remember being rushed to the Department of Children and Families' main office, the 401 Building. The courtyard was busy and filled with a countless number of children to be fingerprinted in the wake of the Rilya Wilson story. Rilya was a toddler in the care of an unauthorized custodian and had gone unseen by the Department for about eighteen months. Her case manager had falsified home visit notes and lied about checking on her safety and well-being. She hadn't seen Rilya in over a year, and, sadly, she was murdered. Although Rilya's body has yet to be found, she left a stain on the system, resulting in the Rilya Wilson Act[3] and privatization of the foster care system. Now, the state contracts with non-profit organizations to provide ongoing case management service to its clients.

It seems my family and I had been unfortunate like Rilya and gotten caught in the crossfires of an overly burdened workforce. All I know for sure is that my life underwent a drastic change on the fourth of October 1996. I was four years old when the Department of Health and Rehabilitative Services (HRS), now the Department of Children and Families (DCF), investigated my family. The child protective investigator determined that my mother lacked protective capacities and my father, John Anthony, was never

---

3   **s. 39.604** — a child from birth to the age of school entry who is under court-ordered protective supervision or in out-of-home care and is enrolled in an early education or childcare program must attend the program 5 days a week unless the court grants an exemption.

a part of my life. The investigation concluded that my parents subjected me to abandonment and neglect, and, in my best interest, I should be legally removed from their care and custody.

The file was nothing more than the documented version of my life. It lacked many pieces of the story, which I know by living it as a child, a young adult, an advocate, and a dependency case manager. This memoir is simply my truth, once and for all.

"You are the designer of your destiny; you are the author of your story."

- Lisa Nichols

CHAPTER ONE

Removal

"You can cry, ain't no shame in it."
   - **Will Smith**

earing the nursery rhyme "Where Is Thumbkin" triggers a blurred, tearful memory. It reminds me of a time when I saw my mother's hands and feet shackled in handcuffs as she was guarded by police officers. While trying to understand the correlation, the full scope of the moment never comes to mind. I have asked questions and heard stories, but everyone I turn to has different versions or hardly remembers anything. It sucks that either I was too young to remember or I suffer from suppressed memory.

My conscious mind stores the reminiscence of being a young girl living at Nile Gardens Apartments in Opa-Locka, Florida with my mother, Gina, and my older siblings, Craig and Ashley. I can't recall the number of bedrooms or the decor of our home. I loved for my hair to be styled with red beads while my arm was accessorized with gold bracelets. I enjoyed playing hide-and-seek and getting into the neighborhood pool with my friends. I followed my mother's rule while playing outside. She had only one: "If you hear gunshots, do not go near the front gate of the apartment complex."

I remember spending one summer with my maternal great-aunt, Auntie Mae, and her husband, Uncle John Henry, in Palm Coast, Florida. During the four-hour drive in my Auntie Mae's cream-colored Lincoln, she described the city like it was a special island. Her stories left me eager to arrive at the destination. Auntie Mae's home was beautiful. It was a mansion in my eyes. The only house on the block, it was surrounded by acres of trees. She told me it was her own special design built from the ground up. It included a two-car garage, garden, walk-in closet, jacuzzi, built-in pool, a lake, and my own room. Uncle John Henry even had his own room outside of the bedroom they shared.

That summer, I learned how to hook bait, fish and scale a fish. I got scared when it jumped. I learned it was taboo to eat with elbows on the table, how to garden and make up a bed. I was introduced to salmon croquettes, southern fried corn, shopping sprees, and Golden Corral Buffet and Grill. Uncle John Henry was the man of the house, and cutting the corn off the cob to make fried corn was a job only for a man. Auntie Mae spoiled me with seasoned T-bone steak any time my taste buds craved for one. I always had to be pretty and dressed in my Sunday's best. It was painful to get my hair done. She would hot comb my hair and blame it on the steam when she burned me, then we'd laugh about it. She'd say, "You have to suffer for beauty" as we admired the pretty sleek ponytails she'd styled in my hair and the sweet scent of Pink Lotion.

I hold those memories near to my heart. They're special to me.

But my return to Miami was unfamiliar. I returned home to chaos. My aunt Shawn screamed as she badgered me, asking if this was the home I wanted to return to. People rampaged through our apartment, taking all our stuff. Some of our belongings were already on the front lawn. We had been evicted. Shawn was aggravated with me and my return to Miami. We all lived in the same apartment complex; her home was just on the other side of the building. She called me a cry baby and left me alone in her apartment.

Gina showed up and tried to find a way to get me out through the window but failed due to its structure. What I didn't know was that she would never be my mother again once she walked away that day. I was too young to grasp what was happening and what was soon to come.

Kids should only be concerned with having fun, watching reruns of their favorite television shows, and eating candy. But not me. My kidulthood started at the age of four. I was making decisions that should have been made by adults because I didn't know a thing about life.

It was the summer of 1996. Unbeknownst to me, what I knew to be a summer vacation was a premeditated safe haven. It made sense. The plan was for me to live with Auntie Mae all along. Gina had been deteriorating as a parent before I'd left for Palm Coast. But I didn't stay in Palm Coast because my cries for my sister, Ashley, were too much to deal with while my auntie and uncle tended to their health. I used to run out of my room screaming, "I want my sister!" At least that's the story Auntie Mae told me before passing away. I wish she hadn't allowed my tears to determine her decision, because returning to Miami resulted in me being removed by social services followed by a slew of custody battles and trauma.

The thought of my parents abandoning me for cocaine and heroin never crossed my mind. My mother's partying and poor money management, my father's absence, and both their drug addictions led the judge to agree with the Department's recommendation—to be legally removed from the custody of both my parents. The judge ordered that I be placed in the custody of Grandma Rose. Ashley told me she had refused to leave the courts without me that day. She didn't want me to be separated from her and Craig.

You never know what life has in store for you . . .

Life as a foster kid does not exempt you from the detrimental environments that the system intends to shield you from. It seems being removed from my parents left me more vulnerable to them.

CHAPTER TWO

Placement One

"Children have never been very good at listening to their elders,
but they have never failed to imitate them."
- James Baldwin

I was living with a non-relative[1] in the heart of Liberty City. Although Grandma Rose was not my biological grandma, she was the only one I knew. Because she wasn't a blood relative, she didn't qualify to receive financial assistance from the State while caring for me, but, still, she was accommodating, never complained, and was willing to care for me to prevent my siblings and me from being separated. We lived in a two-bedroom home with a den. The den was transformed into an extra bedroom, which Ashley and I shared.

My mom never signed me up for school, so Grandma Rose enrolled me into Unific Academy of Learning with the help of the Department, who provided a daycare referral from the Early Learning Coalition to cover the cost of services. Unific was walking distance from our home, so there were no hassles about transportation. I liked the school. They fed us good food for breakfast, lunch, and snack time. Mixed fruits were my favorite. I loved playing kitchen, going to recess, and going on cool field trips. Unific took us to a place with pretty decorations and gifts every year around Christmas time and hosted the most rewarding fundraisers. The student that sold the most chocolate bars earned a place in the annual Martin Luther King Parade. Thanks to Ashley, who sold candy for me, I got to have my moment for making the most sales one year, riding the float, wearing the crown, and

---

1   s. 39.01(52) — **Non-relative**; a person unrelated by blood or marriage or a relative outside the fifth degree of consanguinity.

waving at the people. Even though she was a child herself, she always looked after me. During the madness with our mom and while living with our grandma, she dressed me before school, did my hair in neat ponytails, and made me grilled cheese sandwiches with ham for breakfast. They were always toasted to perfection with crispy, golden trims.

The one thing I hated about school was when our teacher put us in groups to sing along. I cried when it was time to sing "Where Is Thumpkin."

Outside of school, I met new friends in the neighborhood. A typical day for us consisted of playing outside at the park, riding our bikes, getting into the pool at Charles Hadley Park, or climbing mango trees. After climbing trees, we went back on the block to cut our fruit and make mango salads. We ate, talked, and laughed on one of our porches until the streetlights came on, which meant it was time to go into the house.

I was labeled a "grandma's girl." Grandma Rose and I did almost everything together. I was always under her wing as she molded me and imposed her illogical rules on me because I was a girl. She was stricter on girls than boys for some unknown reason.

Grandma Rose lived by a rare rule that women should be out of bed and starting their day by 6 a.m. I never asked her where she'd learned that, but she always enforced it. I'd be up whining to go back to bed while she cooked breakfast and drank her daily mug of coffee. Her coffee was never to my liking. It was nasty, never with enough cream and sugar.

Grandma Rose was a maid. She cleaned houses that looked just like Auntie Mae's. It was the first kind of job I learned about. On days when school was out, I'd tag along and go with her to work. We would catch the bus because driving wasn't her forte, and her boss always picked us up from a specific location. It seemed she knew when I was coming, because she always had a gift for me. I didn't know how she knew; my grandma would randomly ask me if I wanted to go or not.

It didn't dawn on me until I was older why my grandma was cleaning another woman's house. Nobody ever came to our house to clean it, and we ironed our own clothes. Rose is retired now and tends to speak her mind.

She has moments when she says funny things about white folks. "Black folks ain't supposed to be mingling with them people." She's gotten better over time, but knowing what I know now about racism, slavery, and segregation, I don't judge her. She's lived through an era I don't think I would've survived. I just hope her boss's gifts weren't gestures to prep me to clean her house next in case anything happened to Grandma Rose. We never know what life has in store for us, but I never intended to live by the laws of Jim Crow. And Grandma Rose always told me, "Get your education, and don't be working for peanuts like me."

She loved to cook, and I loved to eat. She would have big cookouts for holidays, birthdays, and sometimes no reason at all. Everybody in the neighborhood loved my grandma's cooking. She would take Craig, Ashley, and me shopping, and we all enjoyed it. We rode the Jitney to Downtown Miami and split up once we arrived. I always stayed with Grandma Rose to pick out my clothes. She made sure I had fresh uniforms, stockings, and saddle shoes for school. The day wasn't complete if I didn't get a sausage sandwich from one of the Spanish street vendors. They were so good when grilled to perfection. She knew I loved them, so she never told me no or forgot to buy me one.

When the holiday season came around, I wrote my Christmas list more than fifty times, perfecting my handwriting before giving it to her. Every year, I got exactly what I wanted. For some odd reason, even when I didn't request an Easy-Bake Oven and baby dolls, they still made it under the tree. I never remembered what happened to the oven I'd gotten the prior year. And even though I didn't care for baby dolls, I fought my cousin every year because he'd rip their heads off just to bother me.

The good times came with a price. The number of people living in our house increased over time. There was a time when we lived in a three-bedroom house with more than fourteen people, a mixture of adults and children that caused a bunch of aggravation and drama. If my cousins weren't fighting each other, it was my aunties, Lisa and Tasha, or Grandma Rose and one of her daughters or her son, my uncle Lou. Lou lived in our garage.

He had a drug addiction and use to steal money out of Grandma Rose's purse to feed his addiction. Sometimes she caught him red-handed and was livid. Fights between the boys in the house were just kids being kids, but the fights between Grandma Rose and Tasha were problematic. Tasha had a serious temper, and her anger tended to escalate into pure rage. During one altercation, she grabbed a knife. Grandma Rose often expressed that she feared for her life. She would send me to either of our neighbors' houses as she screamed for help. Sometimes the police showed up to arrest Tasha and haul her off to jail. Other times, she just left until next time.

The more my family fought, the more I began to normalize violence as a response to conflict and an expression of frustration. Besides fighting with cousins, my first street fight was with my childhood best friend, Mya. I don't remember why we fought, but I'm sure it was for a stupid reason. I do remember being praised by my friends and Tasha for beating her up and giving her a black eye. Mya snitched and came to my house with her uncle, crying and holding her eye. I earned myself an ass whooping that day. And Grandma Rose was old school. She would make me pick my own switch off the bush in our front yard and beat me with it. In all fairness, both Mya and I had gotten beat up that day and were back to being friends the next.

My urge to fight didn't stop there. I was a student at Santa Clara Elementary with a few other kids on the block. It wasn't the closest school, so I had to catch a bus that picked us all up at one stop. I was told that a boy who rode the bus with me was bothering one of my friends in school. The next day, I confronted him.

"Do you have a problem?" I asked.

Of course, he jumped up, ready for war. He put up a good fight, and part of me regretted stepping to him, but I was that crazy, so I pulled out a pair of scissors. Before I could stab him, though, other kids grabbed me and broke up the fight.

"You must be brave, bold, and courageous and find a way . . ."
– **John Lewis**

I'll never forget Mr. Jones. He lived alone and was the granddad of our block. When he wasn't interfering in my family's violence, he would babysit me after school when my grandma had business to handle. He'd be right there when I got off the school bus, and he'd fix me an after-school snack and help me with my homework. Other times, the other kids and I went to his home just to chill with him. We'd park our bikes on the sidewalk, sit on his porch, and just talk. Older people love to talk—about anything—so the subjects were always random.

It was a sad day in the neighborhood when he passed away. One day, after returning home from a family outing at Piccadilly's, there was a lot of commotion on the block. Everyone was surrounding Mr. Jones's house, including the fire department. Of course, I rushed over to see what on earth was going on. His daughter was there. She said she had become worried when she hadn't talked to him in a few days. He wasn't answering the door, so they were looking for a way to enter without having to burst through. I was the smallest of the bunch, so they decided to put me through the window to open the front door. I knew Mr. Jones kept his key near the kitchen on a hook hanging from the island.

I figured it was one of two things: Mr. Jones wasn't home, or he was sleeping really hard. Neither were the case. I found him unresponsive, sitting on his living room sofa. I called his name, but he was dead. I paused for a moment. This was the first time I'd ever come face to face with death and the first time I remember my body overheating, palms sweating, and heart racing. I was scared. I wanted to turn back. The thought crossed my mind, but I didn't. I pushed through it for Mr. Jones. I faced my fears and unlocked the courage stored within me.

Fear is an emotion to which we can determine our response. We can allow our fears to hold us back and never discover the what-ifs, or we can choose to face our fears, challenging them head on to reach heights we never dared to imagine. We will never know unless we take the first step.

Despite the dysfunction, I became aware of what it felt like to have a home, family, and good neighbors. I was so comfortable that I didn't think much of my parents. I never yearned for them or wondered why I was living with Grandma Rose. But one day, my living arrangement abruptly ended.

There are two documented home-visit[2] notes in my file; however, I only recall one time a case manager came to my house. Shawn randomly showed up with a lady I had never seen before. The lady identified herself as an employee of the Department of Children and Families, and she was there to remove my brother and me without any new allegations. Oddly enough, other children residing in the home under the Department's supervision, including Ashley, weren't removed. There were rumors that the lady was, in fact, a fraud. She was not the assigned worker to our dependency case. She was Shawn's friend, a mental health social worker, and doing her dirty work so Shawn could gain custody of us to get money from the State.

Ashley told me that one day, she'd overheard Shawn saying she would buy a house with the money if she had custody of us. We were illegally removed and never went before a judge to authorize the placement modification. A court hearing never occurred, and a home study[3] for placement was not completed.

After the move, my brother and I were no longer together. Craig was placed into a separate home with a person who didn't have legal rights to care for him. Grandma Rose didn't have any say in the situation. She was under the impression that she had lost custody of us. She was left terrified. She thought by not giving the worker a hassle and following orders would result

---

2 **Home Visit** — a strategy to assess and monitor the home environment and child's well-being and safety. Workers check to see if the home environment is clean and safe and that the child has appropriate sleeping arrangements, storage space, and follow-up on engagement in services. They also assess for needs. It is required by law and should be held at least every twenty-five days and unannounced every ninety days.

3 **Home Study** — an assessment to evaluate the home and life of a prospective caregiver to determine the appropriateness of a child's placement.

in everything being alright. She was wrong.

I've learned many people are unaware of their rights. Most tend to react out of fear when confronted by a person holding a badge issued by the government. People are willing to do whatever that person instructs them to do to avoid trouble simply because they're a government official hired to do a job. That lack of knowledge subjects us to violations of our rights—and trauma.

CHAPTER THREE
Placement Two

"A child cannot be taught by anyone who despises him, and a child cannot afford to be fooled."
- **James Baldwin**

My placement status changed from non-relative care to relative care. The next two and a half years of my life were spent living with Shawn. Although a case manager had come to remove me from Grandma Rose's house, no case manager supervised me while at Shawn's house.

I was going through several transitions. I was now separated from both my brother and sister and friends, and both my home and school environments had been disrupted. I was transferred to Nathan B. Young Elementary in the middle of the second grade. At first the other students were mean, but soon, as I got comfortable, I was transferred to yet another school, Golden Glades Elementary.

I started the third grade fresh. I met new friends, and I liked my teacher, Ms. Gauthier. She helped me discover my love for reading and strength in writing. In class, we read the Harry Potter and Captain Underpants series. Both were my favorites, so they were must-sees when they came to the big screen.

Reading was a big competition at Golden Glades. My best friends, Steph, Niesha, Nique, and I battled to see who could earn the most points on the accelerated reader program, a program that quizzed us on the content of the books we read. We always went for chapter books because they were worth more points. Golden Glades hosted a reading competition with different award levels based on how many points we earned. I was eager to win, and I did. I reached the highest level and was rewarded with a certificate, a medal, and a trophy. I wish I had kept up with those awards.

But life didn't remain that simple. I became curious about my mother's whereabouts and why I didn't live with her. It was a topic that no one ever discussed and processed with me. Shawn made it hard for me not to think about it, though. It was almost like she wanted me to, and maybe she did.

When I misbehaved, her definition of discipline was a beating and repeatedly yelling, "You're gonna end up just like Gina!" At the time, I didn't know what my mother was, so I couldn't grasp what she expected me to become. From the tone of her voice, I knew it wasn't anything good. Eventually, her verbal abuse grew to be more descriptive, and I started to have more of an idea about why my mother wasn't around and what she was doing in the world.

Shawn's malicious ways escalated from harsh words to physical abuse. She birthed my insecurities and made me feel worthless and undeserving. She predicted that I would never amount to anything. She said, "You will be on drugs, prostituting just like your mama!" as she yelled at me or in the midst of beatings.

I noticed welts all over my body after she'd beaten me, the kind that prevented me from taking a bath because they stung like hell when the water touched them. One time, she grabbed a piece of the vacuum cleaner and beat me with it. I wanted to get away from her, but I didn't know how. I learned to black out when she was beating me or yelling at me.

I found comfort in calling a teenage couple at church Mommy and Daddy. I don't remember their names, but I can still see their faces. Outside of church, we talked on three-way calls. They always asked about my day in school and if I did my homework. Sometimes, like real parents, they'd get on my case about fighting in school and give advice about staying out of trouble and how to stop sucking my thumb, which Shawn taunted me about.

Like Harry Potter, I shared a home with family members who weren't the most welcoming. Sometimes, I'd share a room with Shawn's son, and other times, her daughter. I had to move between bedrooms when her kids wanted their own space. Because my parents weren't in my life, Auntie Mae would send boxes of clothes for me, but I couldn't keep them for myself. Shawn would take most of them and give them to her daughter, Kimberly. One day, while walking home from school, I let all our friends know that Kimberly had on my red Tweety Bird skirt set. Auntie Mae had given it to me, and everything she gave me was special. I don't regret running my mouth, either. I got a beating later that day, but I didn't care; it was worth it. Shawn's daughter had learned how it felt to be embarrassed by me.

Recently, Kimberly found her way onto my Facebook page, telling me not to forget where I came from. I was voicing my opinion about the malicious behavior of Miami-Dade County correctional officers, and her paternal aunt happens to a correctional officer in Broward County. Kimberly's aunt took offense to the post and defended her coworkers. My Facebook friends attacked her on the post due to their own experiences, so Kimberly came to her defense. My anxiety skyrocketed. I grew hot and sweaty and started shaking, which often happens when I get upset. It's like my insides start to boil and the steam is being released through my pores. I hate to be disrespected. I had to let her know that I'll never forget where I came from, but she had better not, either. And she'd be wise to remember why it was in her best interest not to play with me. I almost came out of retirement and nearly called her out to fight. I would have beat her for the old and the new, but instead, I hit the block button. The battle wasn't worth fighting. People sure do try to use your past against you to control, hurt, and devalue you once you've blossomed.

I used to cry to go back to Grandma Rose's house. To get me to change my mind, Shawn would take me to her house and let me spend some time with them. Before dropping me off, we'd sit in the car in front of the house while she highlighted all its dysfunction and lack of structure. Granted, Grandma Rose's house was somewhat out of order because so many people lived there, but it was better than living with Shawn.

Shawn would ask, "Where are you going to sleep?" My judgement was clouded, and I didn't know what was best for me. Even with all my belongings packed, I always ended up back at Shawn's house. Business as usual. There was something about her voice and the instilled fear that kept me from saying what I wanted deep down inside. Thinking about it now, I would have settled for the noise to be away from her and back with Ashley.

Even though I didn't get to spend a lot of time getting to know Gina, a part of me loved her. I guess that was natural. I suffered from a lot of anger and confusion. I couldn't fight Shawn when she spoke bad about my mom, so the anger was released through my behavior at school. I began to have erratic outbursts and became rude and disruptive. I was triggered when my schoolmates made jokes about my mother being a crackhead. They earned themselves a punch to the face. And when I couldn't get to them, I had psychotic episodes, screaming and kicking with tears running down my face. I spent a lot of time in indoor suspension, isolated facing the wall in the principal's office. To assist with managing my emotions and behavior, every Wednesday I was removed from class to participate in art therapy.

I was young and didn't think there was much I could have done to escape. Living with Shawn felt like hell, and the abuse was her way of releasing the hatred and jealousy she had for my mother. All I know about Gina and Shawn's relationship is stories I've heard from others, including the ones Gina shared with me. Everyone told me Shawn was envious of my mother. Gina had been the lucky sibling, with a loving husband, family, and children. She used to own her home and had financial stability.

It was said that when my biological maternal grandmother passed away, she left her house to Shawn. Blessed with financial stability, Gina gave money to Shawn to pay the mortgage. But instead of being responsible, Shawn never made the payments and eventually lost the house. Shawn took me there once. At the time, it was an abandoned property. Auntie Mae said she wished Gina and Shawn had a relationship like her and her own sister, and she always prayed on it.

I got to spend another summer with Auntie Mae and Uncle John Henry before I began middle school. It was the typical fun summer in Palm Coast filled with church, eating, conversation, shopping, fishing, and sharing each other's company. Uncle John Henry sat in his recliner while Auntie Mae and I sat on the sectional sofa that included two end-seat recliners. We would all get comfortable and enjoy our daily television shows like *In the Heat of the Night*, *Columbo*, *The Price Is Right*, *Wheel of Fortune*, and *Jeopardy*.

One evening, we gathered in the living room and watched *Holiday Heart*, a movie about a drag queen named Holiday who took in twelve-year-old Nikki and her drug-addicted mother, Wanda. Auntie Mae said I reminded her of Nikki. After finishing the film, I understood why. I was Nikki, and my mom was Wanda. The movie gave me a clear visual and better understanding of the reality of a young girl losing her mother to drugs.

Auntie Mae was a praying woman, and every night before bed, we got on our knees to say our prayers. Normally, we'd recite Psalms 23. However, after watching the film, her prayers were different. The tone of her voice was tense, and her words changed. She asked the Lord to deliver Gina from drugs and return her home from the streets to care for her daughter.

The next few days held minimal conversation, but I could feel the emotional energy throughout the house. After watching Nikki, Wanda, and Holiday, I found the courage to tell Auntie Mae about what was going on back at home. We always ate meals together, so I decided breakfast was the perfect time. Uncle John Henry listened but rarely did he comment. Auntie Mae was open and listened. It was like she already knew things weren't right.

During the conversation, I learned a few new things. Auntie Mae talked about her bonded relationship with her sister. The way she spoke so highly of my grandma, I knew she had to be a loving lady. I wish I'd had the chance to meet her. And if she were alive, maybe I would've lived with her. But she and my grandfather had passed away before I was born. I also learned that Shawn was receiving financial assistance from the State because I was in her care. It made me question why I was never able to get things I wanted and why she was so cheap. Some would say I should've been grateful for my Payless shoes, but other kids teased me for wearing them. They'd sing, "Payless shoes ain't got no grip; they'll make you fall and bust your lip." Auntie Mae felt that since I was spending the summer with her, the money should've come with me. But not once did Shawn consider the idea.

CHAPTER FOUR

Placement Three

"Whatever someone did to you in the past has no power over the present. Only you give it power."
- **Oprah Winfrey**

Finally, I escaped the wicked witch of the South. I had opened up to Auntie Mae and never had to go back to the place where I felt unwanted and abused.

After spending the summer in Palm Coast with Auntie Mae, I returned to Miami with a new wardrobe to live with my big sister, Ashley, who was now an adult and living on her own with two children. The Department of Children and Families was never contacted. The move was based solely on my desire not to return to Shawn's house. Again, we never went before a judge to legally modify my placement, a home study was not completed, and Ashley didn't gain legal custody to care for me. She mentioned that the State had denied her due to her age. She was twenty-two or twenty-three, and the State didn't believe she had the ability to care for me with two children of her own on her income. I don't know what determining factors they'd considered, because I don't recall a case manager coming to our house to conduct an assessment.

Mysteriously, the file indicated that Shawn had arranged for me to live with Ashley, which was a lie. Her opinion was not included in the decision for me to move out of her home. She wasn't given an option. Had she alerted the Department that she no longer wished to care for me, the appropriate measures to change custody and placement would have occurred. Before I could move to a new home, we would've gone to court, the judge would have ordered that a home study be completed on Ashley's home, the worker would have conducted a home study assessment then made a recommendation for approval or denial to the courts. The judge would have made the final decision to either agree with the Department or override their recommendation, determining the next steps of my life. Had I had the opportunity to share with the Department or a judge what was occurring in Shawn's home, something was warranted to happen. But nothing ever did, and it contradicts Shawn's statement that she had legally relinquished her custodial rights and discontinued all financial assistance she was receiving on my behalf. If she was telling the truth, that means the system knowingly left me without a legal guardian.

At the time, normalcy for children under the supervision of the Department wasn't near normal. Children were not allowed to spend the night, let alone live with a person, even a relative, who hadn't passed a level II background check and a home study, and been issued a court order. This practice is still prohibited, although the Prudent Parent Act[1] was passed into legislation. But somehow, I continued to live with Ashley without any intervention from the Department.

I was happy to be back with my sister. Although we lived in Miami Beach, we spent most of the time at Grandma Rose's house. I was back in my old neighborhood with friends. I was guaranteed simple things like shoes that I liked, appointments to get my hair done, birthday cakes, and Christmas gifts. One Christmas, all I wanted was a radio, and I got it. I had a thing for music and got to listen to the most popular radio station in the city, 97.7 F.M.

Grandma Rose helped us by using the custody order from 1996 to register me for school. My alleged legal guardian didn't help us at all. Shawn didn't want anything to do with us, and the feeling was mutual. I began attending Allapattah Middle School. As part of our daily routine, Ashley, my niece, my nephew, and I would have to wake up extra early to get ready and be on time. We caught three public buses to get to our destinations: the K,

---

1   **s. 409.145 - Care of children, "quality parenting"** — The child welfare system of the department shall operate as a coordinated community-based system of care which empowers all caregivers for children in foster care to provide quality parenting, including approving or disapproving a child's participation in activities based on the caregiver's assessment using the "reasonable and prudent parent" standard.

the J, and the 12 or 21, whichever bus came first.

I was interested in joining the cheerleading squad at school, and I signed up to try out. Every day after school, I went to practice to learn the routines. I remember the rush I felt when the names of the girls who had made the team were posted, including mine. I was an official Mustang. But there was one problem—we didn't have the money to afford the cheerleading uniforms. That dream ended quickly, negating my hard work to make the squad.

With nothing else to do, my behavior went downhill. I began hanging with my friends and skipping class. My sixth-grade year was filled with many unforgettable memories. Everyone arrived at school an hour before it started, which gave us enough time to go to the neighborhood candy lady's house, laugh, and socialize. She sold snacks and food. We ordered chicken and fries, and regardless of how long the line was, we waited for it every morning. I know she made a lot of money with that business.

Throughout the day, we would play fight, the boys vs. the girls. Between classes, if we got caught by one of the crew members, it was on. Then the other crew would have to go back for revenge. We had nothing but fun. For lunch, we hung out and ate chicken again. The school was known for its famous chicken boxes. I ate a box every day with a strawberry shortcake. Early release days were even more fun. We got a thrill out of going to Wendy's to order food just to have a big food fight. Eventually, the restaurant banned students from entering the establishment on early release days.

I had classes with all my friends and never had issues with performing academically when I did attend class. My teachers always said I was smart but needed to improve my behavior. Ashley put me on punishments and banned me from using the house phone. Eventually, she thought the best thing to do was change my environment by removing me from the school. I was devastated.

She transferred me to Nautilus Middle School, a predominately white school located in Miami Beach. I didn't want to be there. I had an altercation my first day. At the lunch table, a girl opened her juice, and it squirted on me.

Everybody at the lunch table gave me a stare that made me feel like she had done it on purpose. She lightly said, "Sorry," and it pissed me off.

I opened my chocolate milk cartoon, threw it on her, and said, "Oops, sorry!" I was ready to fight.

The other students grew rowdy, triggering security to arrive before anything else could happen. But that moment showed the rest of the school that I wasn't to be played with. There were probably no more than twenty black kids attending Nautilus. Over time, I warmed up, and we all became good friends.

I was interested in running track, but I wasn't focused and didn't have the best behavior. I thought even if I was dedicated, everything had a price, and I knew it would be the same as cheerleading. We didn't have the money for that, so I just stopped going after a few practices.

I wasn't the best behaved child, but I loved my sister. I was always jealous when she had a boyfriend or another child. She was getting ready to have her third child, and it felt like my sister was being taken away from me again. I was selfish and wanted my sister all to myself. Even though I was jealous, I had always gotten over it and adjusted to any additions to our family. But this time was different. Something about her new boyfriend just wasn't right, and my spirit knew it. There was a demon among us, and Ashley went from being my hero to the devil's advocate.

This guy was precise and strategic. His tactic was simple: If he could ruin the relationship between my sister and me, he would have his way. On days we didn't have school, my friends and I talked on the phone for hours, always with at least four of us on the phone at a time. Sometimes, we got on the party line just for fun. Sometimes, I called in from my phone because everyone else's line was tied up due to three-way calling. Once I was done with the call, this weirdo would push the redial button to see who I was talking to. With no circumstantial or hard evidence, he tried to convince my sister that I was having sex with older men. I was a virgin. The thought of sex wasn't nearly on my mind. I didn't even think I was pretty enough for boys to like me. I just found joy in hanging with my friends, doing fun stuff that wasn't always good but never chasing behind boys.

He taunted me about the fact that my mother had abandoned me for drugs. He called her a crackhead and said she didn't love or want me—but he never said it when my sister could hear him. I started to yearn for my mother. I wished she was there to protect me. He escalated to attacking my self-esteem by calling me ugly and picking at my dark skin color and the scar on my lip from falling off a bike when I was younger. It had left a lump the doctor said was scarred tissue. Shawn told me if I didn't stop sucking my thumb, the scar wouldn't go away. Stupidly, I thought there could have been some truth to that.

I hated that man. My only wish was that he'd disappear and never come back. I told my sister and Auntie Mae, but I couldn't tell if they believed me. They constantly told me he was an adult, and I had to respect him. I was afraid of him and eventually started running away from home. Each time, I explained to my sister my reason for running away. She promised when I came home things would change. I couldn't stay at my friend's house forever, so I had no other choice but to return home. But nothing ever changed when I did.

Some weekends, Ashley allowed me to spend the night at my friend Ivy's house. Ivy's mom was a licensed foster parent. I wished she had let me always stay with them, but I only got to spend weekends at their house. It seemed like the weekend flew by too fast. When Sunday came, that meant it was time to go home and be with the devil. I dreaded having to leave.

My wish for him to leave never came true, so it made sense for me to act as if he didn't exist. The plan was to treat him like an elephant in the room and just stay out of the way. However, that was still unacceptable, as he demanded to be acknowledged. And sure enough, Ashley agreed.

I started to enter a dark space and gravitated toward a fetish for the color black. The emo lifestyle was attractive. I grew overwhelmed with just existing and found myself contemplating suicide. I was tired of bearing heavy pains, thoughts, and emotions. I would stare at myself in the mirror while I swallowed pills stored in the medicine cabinet, hoping to overdose and die. I imagined myself being rushed to the hospital, getting my stomach pumped but ultimately dying so I wouldn't have to be a burden to people anymore. I learned a lot of it from watching Lifetime. I guess I didn't do it right because none of that ever happened. I learned about other kids who cut themselves. They claimed the feeling helped them cope with their emotions, but I couldn't imagine myself cutting. It sounded too painful. If I had taken my own life, it would've been quick and painless.

Things didn't get better. His behavior escalated. I am a light sleeper. If a penny drops near me, I'll hear it. Some nights, he entered my room. I pretended to still be asleep as I watched him through squinted eyes stand at the foot of my bed with no purpose. He would take a peep out the window and eventually leave.

One morning, as I got dressed for school, I walked down the hallway to my niece and nephew's room. I was left in disbelief and disgust as I saw him use the restroom with the door open. He was urinating, holding his penis in his left hand. I stayed in the kids' room until I knew for sure he had returned to his own and the door was closed. I sat at the breakfast table at school that morning thinking about what had happened as my left eye twitched. It was my intuition speaking. I had a feeling something bad was soon to happen.

It was the last day of eighth grade. As I prepared for school, I heard his voice call my name. Thinking of my sister's orders, I respectfully answered him. "What?" But my response wasn't good enough. He insisted that I get up and come to see what he wanted. I sucked my teeth and rolled my eyes.

Stomping my feet, I approached the door to his room, and my body froze. My mouth became instantly dry. I couldn't get a word out. I was in a state of shock. The devil had struck. It seemed so unreal, but he was standing there caressing his erect penis right before my virgin eyes. He reached for me, grabbed my breast, and offered to give me lunch money for school every day.

I didn't respond to his offer. My body finally awakened, and I raced out of the house like lightning. I ran as fast as I could down the flight of stairs and into the street to the school bus stop. Out of breath, I told my friends what had just happened. I used my friend's cell phone to call my sister but didn't get an answer. I called her best friend, who questioned if I was telling the truth. I provided her a straight answer. "Yes!"

She said she'd try to contact Ashley. I called Ivy's mom as well and stayed on the phone with her until the police got involved. I told the bus driver, and I rode the school bus until the police came to retrieve me. They drove me back to my house. From inside the car, the officer instructed me to identify the man who had just attempted to rape me. I confirmed it was him. He was handcuffed, and the officer hauled him off to jail.

I gave my statement to the police several times: in the car on the corner of my house, during the ride to the station, and many more times at the station. Everything happened so fast. After questioning, I was returned to Ashley, who had waited for me in the lobby.

She began her own questioning. "Did it really happen?"

"YES!" I said.

Her next statement caught me off guard. "I wonder if I can change my statement." At that moment, I knew she didn't believe me.

A few months later, when I was no longer living with her, I gave her a call. It was heavy on my mind. I needed to know if she believed me. On the call, she claimed she did, but I was confused because he still lived with her and I didn't. I thought about my niece. She was still a little girl, and I could only pray he didn't try anything with her.

The police didn't believe me either, or they just didn't do anything about it. The officer gave clear instructions: He and I were not to be in proximity. We left the station, and that was it. There were no further repercussions for his actions. Even the law had failed to protect me.

After the incident, I saw him on three different occasions. Stupidly, he spoke every time. Two out of the three times, I responded in anger, becoming emotionally unhinged because he had the audacity to speak to me after what he had done. The first time, I cursed him out and later drowned myself in tears. The second time, my anger went haywire as I released derogatory language from my mouth. The third time, I like to think I showed improvement.

While I was getting my hair done, he said, "Money, is that you?"

I calmly humiliated him by letting everyone in the barber shop know that he was a grown man who liked little girls.

My last words to him: "Stop fucking speaking to me, *rapist!*"

He did the same thing every time, smirked and said, "Yeah, that's Money" and walked away.

Money is my nickname. Gina gave it to me. Ashley told me Gina had saved up a ton of my boo-boo pampers to throw at John for being a deadbeat dad. As she threw them, she said, "She doesn't need none of your money. She gonna have her own!" and she nicknamed me Money.

A few months before the incident with Ashley's boyfriend, Gina had called out of the blue and said she was in drug rehabilitation. She was drug free and wanted to be back in our lives. I started spending every weekend at her house. When the officer said Ashley's boyfriend and I couldn't be in the same house, I knew exactly where I was headed—to my mom. I called her to tell her about my day. It felt good to be able to run to her, especially at a time like this one.

On my usual route, I caught the K and J buses to the Allapattah Metro Rail Station to catch the south train to Perrine. But something was off. Even though my mom knew I was on my way, she wasn't there when I arrived. And travel time had taken a couple hours. I sat outside in her boyfriend's parked car waiting for her. I repeatedly called her phone. She sporadically answered and reassured me she was on her way, but one hour turned to two, and two turned to three. Time continued to pass until, eventually, nighttime fell.

After several exhausting hours of waiting, she arrived. I tried talking to her more in depth about what had happened, but her reaction was more than strange. She didn't show any kind of affection and seemed to be withdrawn and disinterested in having any form of conversation. I came to my senses, stopped trying, grabbed a blanket, and laid on the couch crying myself to sleep.

She was acting careless like all the others. I was worried that it was because of one of two things—either she really didn't care or had relapsed. She never provided an explanation for what had taken her so long to come home.

The next day, a child protective investigator (CPI) came to visit us. He told us that, legally, we were not supposed to be together. I couldn't be with my mother or go back to my sister's. As I look back at the situation, I wonder why the investigator didn't take me with him. That would have been the most appropriate thing to do.

The Department was aware of the molestation incident, as it is documented in the file. But it doesn't mention anything about the CPI visiting and interviewing Gina and me. At the time, my family presented a serious need for intervention again. I wasn't safe. I needed someone to protect me. I didn't have a permanent place to stay and had just reported an incident of sexual assault. My family was already known to the Department. And when they showed up, I hadn't been in the care and custody of the guardian their records claimed the courts had appointed since 1996. It was now 2008.

In fact, this should have been a new case of abandonment and neglect against Shawn. I was living with my sister, who had been allegedly denied the right to become my legal guardian. I was seen with my mother unsupervised, and she didn't have the legal right to be anywhere near me. I didn't even have a stable home. The investigative summary for the case states that I was a liar, that I made things up in my head, and that I was recommended for a psychological evaluation, allegations the Department failed to look further into for unknown reasons.

I wasn't crazy, but still, there was a lot going on. The CPI had every ground to proceed with a dependency case but chose to close the case with no indicators. The reports stated that I continued to engage in therapy. That was another lie; I was not participating in any form of therapy at the time.

In the meantime, I stayed with a friend. Her mom agreed to allow me to stay with them until I figured out my next move. I was fourteen years old without a permanent home, mother, or guardian, or guidance from anyone. It was just my little ole self in this huge world, trying to find my way. I was lost, and just living stressed me out even more. Waking up to live life every day was hard. I was under the impression no one loved or cared about me. If my own mother had left and failed to protect and care for me, why on earth would anyone else? It was a motto I stuck with for a long time, helping me cope when others treated me poorly. I expected it because that was the norm in my world.

CHAPTER FIVE

Placement Four

"If you're treated a certain way, you become a certain kind of person."
- James Baldwin

I t was a hot day, a perfect day to get wet, so I decided to get into the pool at Charles Hadley Park. Coincidentally, I ran into one of my first cousins, Tiffany. I asked her to call her mom, Jasmine, to ask if I could live with them. She said yes, and I found my next home with her, her four daughters, her god-sister, and her boyfriend. My file includes awareness of this move, but, of course, we never went before the courts. Even though my cousin took me in, it wasn't legal, and she didn't have custody of me.

I remember her rambling about the State denying her legal custody of me due to her criminal record. I don't know what process she underwent to be denied because a case worker never came to our house to speak to me or conduct any kind of assessment. She had a criminal rap sheet that would have never allowed her clearance for permanency by the courts, and her crimes were too recent. Based on her record, they would feel she was a risk. If they had closed the case with a child in her care, most likely, the child would return to the system.

But for now, with her was where I called home, in a well-known neighborhood called Brownsubs on the second floor of the third building in the Pink and Grays apartments. I don't know how it got its name; the building wasn't pink or gray. There was something always happening there. A normal day was full of fun, drug deals, fighting, shoplifting, drug raids, and shootouts or gun shots for no specific reason, probably young boys just happy to pull a trigger.

Jasmine conducted her home with little restriction. She tended to act more like a friend than a parent. She had one rule: know that she didn't have any money and we were to find a man to take care of us. I couldn't be sure if she was serious or playing. Why would she say something like that to a child? She was known for saying the wildest things, like if we had acne, she recommended letting a man nut on our faces to clear it up. She thought saying things like that was funny, but it wasn't. It made me uncomfortable.

It was the Fourth of July, and Jasmine came home with something for everyone to wear to celebrate the holiday. I waited for her to call my name and give me my clothes, but instead, I found myself asking for mine.

She said, "Oh, shit, I forgot you lived here."

She did give me money to rush to the store to buy clothes, but I still felt left out. Not only had she warned me I would need to find a way to care for myself, but she was already forgetting about me.

With my disinterest in dating men who had the money to take care of me, shoplifting became an appealing means to get the things I needed. I grew to be a frequent thief with only a few instances of getting caught. Sometimes, when I knew I was about to get caught, I'd ditch the stuff before leaving the store. Other times, I wasn't so slick but managed to still get away. After being approached by a secret shopper, one of my stealing escapades ended with me fleeing from Wally World to the back of a meat store. I changed into a pair of pajamas I had just boosted to disguise myself and avoid being arrested. I had a backpack filled with bras, panties, clothes, and hygiene products. I begged the store clerk not to snitch as I saw the police passing in a patrol car. I got away.

Jasmine had legal troubles of her own. One early morning, as I got dressed for school, there was a hard knock on the door. I thought it was Tiffany's friend who picked her up every morning for school. I always yelled at him for knocking on the door so hard. But that morning, it wasn't him; it was the police and federal agents demanding that we open the door. Disobeying their order, I woke Jasmine up to tell her the police were at the door, but before she could open it, the agents, dressed in all black and equipped with big guns, were already in our home.

My hands were up as agents walked into our rooms and put big, long guns with flashlights in our faces. They cuffed and hauled Jasmine off to jail for her crimes.

"I had to grow to love my body. I did not have a good self-image at first. Finally, it occurred to me; I'm either going to love me or hate me. And I chose to love myself. Then everything sprung from there. Things that I thought weren't attractive became sexy. Confidence makes you sexy."
— **Queen Latifah**

Jasmine's boyfriend, Lucas, was harder on me than the other kids in the house. He has since passed away. If Tiffany stayed out late or went to the club without me, I would be punished as if I had control over her actions. If I misbehaved in school, I was punished and forced to do chores while the other children got slaps on the wrist. Every time I post an accomplishment on social media, one of his friends leaves a comment, claiming that he believed in me and knew I would be the one to make it. Some would say people tend to be hard on the ones they believe in, but there's a certain way to do things. It didn't feel like he believed in me. He never told me or showed me that belief while he was living. So why should I believe that? If so, maybe I would have thought differently about myself.

Tiffany was light-skinned with a nice shape, big butt, and a pretty face. She only gave attention to men who could financially care for her. She was the typical "city girl." Guys drooled over her, and even to this day, they ask me about her whereabouts. She was cherished because, of course, she was Jasmine's child, men were attracted to her, and guys took care of her and gave her money, from which Jasmine and Lucas also benefited. Because I wasn't built to deal with guys just for money, I was assigned to protect her, and I got into trouble whenever they felt I didn't.

Their highly favored praises to her caused me to feel insecure about my own beauty. I carelessly lost my virginity to a guy I cared nothing about, even ditching him after the fact. As much as Tiffany boasted about sex, it turned out to be an activity I could do without. I really was the kind of child who found pleasure in doing other things. Boyfriend and girlfriend stuff never hyped me up, or maybe the lack of arousal stemmed from how I felt about myself.

I'm dark-skinned and skinny with a petite frame. I was taunted about being ugly and black and called "bubble lip" due to my scar. If I could have wished upon a star, I would've wished to be separated from my looks. I felt ugly. I thought if I were lighter, prettier, and had a thicker figure, people would like me. I even put bleach in my bath water, thinking it would lighten my complexion. I was always doing something crazy that never worked. I would've later been upset had it worked or caused damage because I eventually grew to love myself and my melanin.

Although I never got praise for my looks, I had a different beneficial skill—I wasn't afraid to fight, so when Tiffany had issues with other girls, I had to fight them. Even if she fought, I did as well. Sometimes, when I didn't want to fight, they'd call me scary, so I'd fight to prove I wasn't. I was in high school fighting middle school kids. I've never looked my age, always younger. It was simple; I would travel to her school, meet up with her once the bell rang, she'd point out the girl, and I'd attack her.

I was mad because one fight caused me to lose one of my pullout gold teeth I had just gotten for Christmas. Tiffany had gotten into an altercation with a girl during school. So once the bell rang, I walked toward Carol City Middle to see what was going on. Tiffany and the girl intercepted my walk because they were already on their way to my school—Miami Carol City High. I spotted them on the corner of a nearby street. I proceeded to fight the girl but was interrupted when the police came. Of course, I ran to get away. I don't know how I managed to jump the tall gate into the nearest apartments, but, somehow, I did, and that's when my gold tooth fell out of my mouth and into the dirt.

I don't remember how Tiffany and I split up. My only thought as I ran through the apartment complex was to escape the police. I heard a scream. It was Tiffany. The girl had caught her off guard and sprayed her in the face with mace. To relieve the pain, a good Samaritan immediately drowned Tiffany's eyes with milk. Milk is the medicine for mace. She was lucky someone was there to help her.

The incident escalated. Later that evening, we went to Lincoln Field

Apartments to fight the girl's cousin. I had to fight her five times, different rounds of fist fighting back to back and on different occasions. After the fight during spring break, she came to my school unexpectedly. Like any other day, I walked to the Green Store, a popular convenience store in Carol City where students congregated after school. Before I made it to the store, she hit me off guard, pulling my head down by my long plaits. I didn't know who had attacked me until the fight was broken up and I asked, "Who hit me?"

It was her. She had come all the way to my school to fight me again. Still, I had to stand my ground. We fought again and again. I didn't have a problem with the girl. I didn't even know her. I was in that mess because of Tiffany, who wasn't even there.

Defending Tiffany led to my first arrest and experience in juvenile detention. Tiffany had been telling me for days that a girl was bothering her. As the end of the school year approached, I finally went to her school. She pointed the girl out, and I attacked her.

In the midst of the beating, Tiffany's encouraging chants changed to screaming. "They coming, Money. Let's go!" she yelled.

I hit the girl a few more times, leaving her on the ground with her peers laughing. I ran and dived into the backseat of the getaway car. Amber, a close family friend, was driving. She sped away as the police chased us, but they eventually stopped because we had crossed county lines.

There was a rumor that the girl had pressed charges and a warrant was issued for my arrest, but I doubted how truthful it was. The girl didn't know my real name, and the authorities never came to our house, so I didn't think much of it. But a few weeks later, Tiff and I were in the back of a police car making jokes on our way to jail for battery and fleeing the scene of a crime.

When situations arose, I had a careless demeanor. Lucas was curious and often questioned me about being depressed. He wondered why I slept so much. Sleep was my way of escaping reality. I was numb when I was asleep. Being careless made it easier for me to adapt to any circumstance, including jail. On the other hand, Tiffany was bugging out. The officers moved her to an isolated cell. When interviewed, she told the counselor she was hallucinating, seeing and hearing people. I swear, the girl had a fetish for attention or was mentally challenged.

We were locked up until about 3 a.m. The process took forever. When we were finally released, all I wanted was my next meal. The jungle juice and sandwich the jail had served us weren't enough. I was hungry.

The judge ordered me to participate in an anger management program and complete community service hours. He recognized my lack of respect for authority, my carelessness, and my bad attitude through my body language. He demanded that I show respect in his courtroom. At the podium, he instructed me to fix my posture and stand up straight while he was speaking to me. I moved from leaning on the podium to tilting my head and folding my arms with my hip to the side, sucking my teeth and rolling my eyes. My attitude earned me an additional six weeks in anger management, six weeks more than Tiffany. If I was angry, the only reason was that I was in trouble for having to fight her battles. I didn't have to worry about the community service hours because one of Lucas's friends was the CEO of a non-profit organization, and he agreed to sign-off on community service hours I never completed.

"A drunk mind speaks a sober heart."
– Jean-Jacques Rousseau

I had my first taste of alcohol at fourteen and first got wasted at fifteen. Tiffany and I would battle for who could drink the most. I'd fill sixteen-ounce red plastic cups to the rim and take them to the head. Other times, we'd battle for who could take the most shots. After a few straight shots of Grey Goose, my heart was on my sleeve, and I expressed myself freely for the first time. Jasmine had let us drink, and my night ended in the tub with cold water running out of the shower head to sober me up.

I had been rolling on the ground outside with tears streaming down my face, repeatedly screaming, "I want my mama!"

I remember Lucas saying, "I told y'all that liquor will bring it out."

Jasmine bragged about how much she loved her auntie—my mom. She always talked about the way Gina cared for her when she was younger. Gina couldn't do wrong in her eyes. She always said, "Regardless, that is still your mother."

I didn't feel the same. It made me even angrier that she had gotten to experience my mother's love and I didn't. I felt she was rubbing it in my face. She kept telling me that for what? What could I do with the information? Her love for my mother allowed an open-door policy, regardless of how many times Gina messed up.

Gina was on another "I'm clean" rodeo. She was court ordered into an inpatient drug program at Spectrum Programs Inc. Even though I had screamed for my mother while I was drunk, the sober me didn't want anything to do with her. I was afraid of being disappointed yet again, but Jasmine didn't leave any room for other options.

On visitation days, we visited her as a family. We all sat outside at a patio table and talked for a few hours. I never had much to say. But just being there made Gina happy. She showed us off to the other residents and bragged that I was her daughter. "This is my baby girl, y'all," she'd say.

I could tell she took pride in the work she was doing to overcome her addiction as she gave me a tour of the facility. She showed me her therapy area, pictures she had colored, and quotes she relied on to maintain her sobriety. For the first time, in the privacy of her room, we got to have a real conversation about what led her to a life of drugs and abandoning her children.

While in the program, Gina took advantage of the beauty of journaling. Her journal was useful as a tool to guide our conversation. Reading a few pages, Gina told me she had reached out to her sister for help to get off the streets once, but Shawn had turned her back on her, pushing her deeper into depression and drug dependency. Instead of helping her, Shawn had closed the door in her face and told her to never come back.

I heard what she said, but I also heard, "I knew where you were, and I never once came to see you," but I didn't interrupt her.

Gina continued and expressed that she had pure hatred in her heart for her sister. Any time she spoke of her it was with hostility and rage. She never held back from saying, "She's dead to me."

She explained that after her husband died, she became dependent on drugs because she couldn't find a way to cope with life.

"But what about your children? What about me?" I asked her.

"I didn't know how to live without him."

I thought, *So I don't have a mother because you loved a man*. A man she spoke so highly about, a loving husband and father, who had left behind a home, children, financial benefits, and a lifetime of good memories for her to hold on to and cherish forever.

She showed me pictures of herself over the years. The pictures showed her smiling with jewelry, money, cars, and clothes. She bragged about earning money from trafficking drugs. I realized she wasn't anything like Wanda on *Holiday Heart*. She had been a functional drug addict who couldn't cope with the passing of her husband but had the will to continue living a lavish lifestyle rather than be a mother. And she had the audacity to tell me all about it.

The hope I'd had for forgiving my mother died. Her answers weren't good enough for me.

With progress and good behavior in the program, she earned off-campus privileges, spending a few hours or, on some occasions, the night at my house. I wanted her far away from me. It bothered me deeply in my soul when she tried to boss me around. It was like she just did it to feel empowered. For no specific reason, she demanded that we put our cellphones on the ironing board at 9 p.m. and go to sleep.

Oh, now you want to be a mother? I just looked at her and rolled my eyes.

Eventually, she graduated from the drug program, maintained her job as a janitor at a nearby elementary school, and moved into an apartment with her boyfriend, Bruce, an older white guy she'd met in the program. He had overcome a drug addiction as well. He sold her dreams about being rich and taking care of her, and the poor lady fell for it.

Jasmine was moving to a new home in Coral Springs and told me I had to go stay with Gina. I didn't want to go but, again, she left me without any other option. Reluctantly, I moved with my mom. Even though I resented her, things weren't all that bad. I had my own room, a computer, and the Internet. I learned that my mom could cook. My favorite meal was her famous fried chicken, pork and beans, and rice. Together, we went on outings to nearby shopping plazas. Even going to the grocery store was considered quality time because we had to catch public transportation and figure out a creative way to carry the bags.

But just when I had let down my guard, Rent-A-Center was in my room dismantling my bedroom set for repossession. Bruce had been lying about paying the monthly bill. The energy in the house shifted. Gina was furious, and she yelled and fussed at Bruce for the rest of the night. I almost puked when she mentioned that he couldn't get it up in the bedroom. *Ew, lady, do you not see me standing here? Have some respect. I can hear you.*

Bruce had relapsed. He was getting high and spending all his paycheck on drugs. He didn't have any of the generational wealth he'd wooed her with.

Tell me something I don't know. The story changed to how, allegedly, his family wouldn't give him his share of the wealth due to his drug addiction. While that may have been true in other families and addiction cases, it didn't apply to Bruce. The clues were evident; he'd graduated from the same program as Gina, so where was his family and their riches? They never visited him, encouraged him, or showed him any kind of support. She was so naïve.

The little hope I'd gained for having a positive relationship with my mother died again. She failed miserably at raising me, her own child. No matter how much hell she raised, the fact remained that she couldn't care for me. My bed became the living room couch due to her dependency on yet another man. Any hope that she couldn't be solely dependent on a man was non-existent. Having support is nice, but it doesn't matter how much a person says they have your back; you must make sure you have your own back first.

Bruce left for good, and it was just Gina and me for a short period. A side of me thought she'd gotten rid of him because she didn't want to relapse. But that was only a thought. Before I could blink my eyes, another man was in our house, her old boyfriend, Frank, the one who had lived with her down south during her last episode of recovery. He was no better than Bruce. He was a drug dealer! Cocaine packages in colorful miniature bags littered our house. They were so disrespectful; they didn't even try to hide it.

I didn't have much of anything to say to her. I drifted off into my own world, doing my own thing, hanging with my friends and even getting my gang name tattooed on my right shoulder: TBB for Taliban Blood Bitches. When she found out, she was furious, but who was she to tell me what to do? I had more fun and felt more love from them than I'd ever felt with her.

Every day was the same routine. I went to school while she went to work. I would get home first and wait for her to come home. The job was next door to our apartment, so she usually arrived home at exactly five o'clock. But one day, things were different. Hours passed, and she hadn't returned home from work. I thought maybe she'd gone to the store. But the more time passed, the more I worried. I repeatedly called and sent text messages. The phone continued to ring, so I knew it wasn't dead. She had to have seen me calling and just decided not to pick up.

Days went by, and there was still no sign of her. She hadn't returned any of my phone calls or text messages. After a while, Frank showed up. I let him know that Gina hadn't been home in a few days and wasn't answering her phone. She was missing.

"Damn, let's go," he uttered and grabbed his car key. He knew where we could most likely find her.

We got into the car and drove to the Triangle, a known spot for drugs in Opa-Locka, to hopefully find her. We searched block by block and at corner stores, asking active groups of people hanging outside and at popular houses where he knew she hung out. I sat in the car while he questioned people and went into the homes. We didn't have any luck that night. Something told me that Frank did find her inside one of the houses, but he didn't want to tell me because she was back on drugs. A part of me respects him for that. He never confirmed it; it's just a gut feeling I had.

There was no food in the house, the utility bills were past due, and there was a final eviction notice on the door. Frank had the audacity to give me the past-due light bill. I was only sixteen years old. I didn't have any money or the slightest idea about how to pay a bill. I contacted Jasmine and Auntie Mae to update them. I don't recall them saying much of anything. I thought Jasmine would've rushed to the scene since she'd forced me to move in with Gina.

I went to stay with my other cousin (not blood related) in Lincoln Field. She didn't sign up to be my caregiver, just allowed me to stay at her house until the situation was sorted out.

I don't remember how much time had passed, but Gina finally decided to resurface. I immediately got on the next 62 bus to go home. Upon her return, she had a plan: get her belongings, dismiss all questions, and leave. I had two questions for her: "Where were you," and "Why would you leave me?" But she ignored my questions. All she did was complain about nobody helping her. She didn't explain what she needed help with. I was confused.

She showed zero interest in continuing motherhood and complained like she was the child.

It pierced my soul to experience abandonment and neglect yet again. I felt that more people played a role in it this time. I had been forced into a situation that I knew couldn't possibly end well, because I had been down the same road before. But people ignored the facts and seemed so eager to get rid of me that they didn't think twice when the opportunity presented itself, even if it meant leaving me with a mother when no one could be sure if she was going to keep her act together. They didn't even care to ensure a backup plan if all failed. It was clear to me that Gina didn't want to be a mother. I just wish others had accepted that fact before I was left to carry the heavy burden of resentment by my lonesome.

I meant it this time around—I was fed up with trying to have a relationship with her. She had given me more than enough ammunition to keep my word.

CHAPTER SIX

Placements Five, Six, Seven, & Eight

"I didn't have anybody, really no foundation in life, so I had to make my own way."
- Tina Turner

M y life was in a gray area. I was just getting by, couch surfing at friends' houses. I continued school at D.A. Dorsey Educational Center, but I rarely went to class and didn't earn any credits. I cried. I didn't know what I was going to do. Life never failed at showing me I didn't matter.

Although Jasmine eventually came and got me, the stay at her house wouldn't be for long. She was finally sentenced to two years in prison for the same crime that had caused the federal agents to rush our house at 5:30 a.m. Before she left to turn herself in, we all stood in a circle, held hands, and prayed as a family. We had never done that before. I guess that was a prayer for all of us to be strong for our own reasons.

Maybe she forgot about me again because she failed to make proper living arrangements for me during her absence. I was left in the care of Lucas, who didn't want me living with him, reasoning that I would lie and say he had inappropriately touched me. Ironically, one of Jasmine's daughters admitted that she had run away at a young age because he was touching her. So maybe his fear had more to do with what he thought of himself versus the possibility of me lying about him.

To get me out of his hair quickly, he shipped me off to live with Amber, a close family friend. Jasmine had arranged for Tiffany to live with Amber before she went to prison. However, the plan didn't work out, because I wasn't into guys how they were, and they said I would only slow them down and they would have to take care of me. Honestly, they were right. I didn't too much like hanging with them, anyway. They liked to hang out at a place they called the bando. The only bando I knew of was an abandoned house, but this place wasn't rundown or boarded up. It was a chill spot. I would sit in the living room while they had sex with their boyfriends in other parts of the house.

One time, my heart pounded outside of my chest as a third guy joined me in the living room while they tended to their business. I didn't know what they had told him, but I hoped he didn't expect to have sex with me. He didn't try anything, thankfully. He asked me a question, and, from the tone of my voice, he must've sensed that I was not into whatever they had going on.

Hanging with them was dangerous. One late evening, a split-second decision not to ride with them possibly saved my life. While riding with one of the guys from the bando, their car was riddled with bullets. Amber was shot and crashed into another car, ending their chances of getting away from the shooter. Spooky, a guy Tiffany was dating, was shot in the back and passed out in the backseat of the car. Tiffany had been grazed several times and remembered the shooter standing over the car emptying the clip with the intent to commit murder. After the shooter left, she tried to get help from nearby residents, but they only screamed, directing her to get off their property.

At the scene, I could only imagine what could've happened to me had I taken that ride with them. I wondered how I was content with going to parties and neighborhood jams and hanging in areas that caused me to duck bullets to stay alive. I never turned down a good time, even knowing that at the last party someone I knew, someone I knew of, or a stranger had been gunned down. Knowing I'd vividly seen blood leak from their bodies and watched as their lives slipped away.

When Tiffany said she didn't want me living with them, it sucked because I didn't have anywhere else to go, but it probably was God's way of keeping me safe. Tiffany had issues. She worried that every time she was close with someone I'd come around and take them away from her.

Family and non-family members continued to debate about who would care for me next. No one really wanted the responsibility. I thought, *Damn, am I really that bad?* Amid all the fuss, Jasmine's best friend, Brooke, stepped up to the plate. She ceased the commotion by emphasizing that, regardless of everything, I was still a child. Jasmine had planned for another one of her daughters to live with her already, so she agreed that I could come, too.

A huge barrier hindered a smooth transition. As she tried to register me for school, it was discovered that I didn't have a legal guardian. Miami Edison Senior High refused to allow me to be registered in school without the proper paperwork. I questioned Lucas about how they were able to register me at Carol City High. He claimed to have known someone in the registration office. So, an anonymous person had allowed the school to register me without having legal guardianship paperwork? Okay.

With Shawn as the biggest cheerleader, she and Jasmine encouraged me to get a GED versus returning to regular school. Jasmine thought it was best for me to go off to job corp. But even though they continued to nag me, something inside me just didn't want a GED. No matter how many times they said, "You know you don't want to go to school," it didn't change my mind. I had the brains to finish high school, and getting a GED was unnecessary. High school was the only factor still associating me with being a child. If I received any kind of diploma, they would have the ammunition to label me an adult, relieving themselves from guilt and responsibility, even though I was only sixteen years old.

In an effort to resolve the matter, Brooke and I called the abuse hotline at 1-800-96-ABUSE. Despite what we reported the reporter heard something different and documented a few wrong details,

When Kenisha was 11, the biological mom, Regina Walker lost custody of her because she was on drugs and out on the streets. Legal guardianship was given to the mom's sister. Five years ago, the aunt would not allow Kenisha to remain in her home. Kenisha was then cared for by a cousin for several years. Recently the cousin was incarcerated. A family friend has been caring for Kenisha, but has not been able to enroll her in school. There is no documentation which gives the friend

authority to act for the child. The aunt was unable to provide any documentation
to enroll the child in school. It is believed that the aunt receives financial support
for the child although she has not lived in the aunt's home for several years. There
is concerns for inadequate supervision for the child.

The report was accepted, and within twenty-four hours, a child protective investigator came out to commence his case. Upon completion of the investigation, he verified findings of inadequate supervision and abandonment against Shawn. She had lied about legally relinquishing her custodial rights. And if she had lied about that, I know, for sure, she had also lied about discontinuing monetary benefits for me all those years. In the unlikely event that she wasn't lying, it meant state workers had continuously falsified legal documents, leaving me in a limbo. The truth will never be known.

This time, things were getting done the right way. The Department went before a judge with a positive home study and recommended I be placed in the custody of a non-relative. Court went so fast that I didn't grasp everything that happened during the hearing, but I knew the judge had granted the Department's wishes and ruled that I be legally placed in Brooke's care and custody with a case plan goal of another planned permanent living arrangement (APPLA).[1]

We spent the summer adhering to most of the judge's orders and the recommendations made by the level of care assessor.

The recommendations were as follows:

1. It is recommended that Kenisha remain in her current placement as her basic needs are met within a safe environment.
2. It is recommended that Kenisha not have any contact with her

---

1 **APPLA** — the least preferred permanency option, "planned" means the arrangement is intended, designed, considered, or deliberate. "Permanent" means enduring, lasting, or stable. The term "living arrangement" includes not only the physical placement of the child or young adult, it also considers quality of care, stability, supervision, and nurturing a youth will receive.

biological parents until they have completed a mental health assessment and substance abuse evaluation to determine their level of functioning. Visitation shouldn't commence until they have demonstrated sobriety through random drug screenings.

3. It is recommended that Kenisha continue to have unsupervised contact with family members with which she maintains good relationships. No contact between Kenisha and prior sexual abuse perpetrators.

4. It is recommended that Kenisha be appointed a guardian ad litem as she currently does not have a permanent guardian to access her needs and ensure those needs are met.

5. It is recommended that Kenisha participate in a mental health assessment to determine her level of functioning given her history of problem behaviors, multiple placements, and issues involving prior abuse/neglect and parents' substance abuse and criminal histories.

6. It is recommended that Kenisha be referred to an independent living program for placement and independent living courses due to her upcoming seventeenth birthday, as reunification is not an immediate case plan goal.

7. It is recommended that the full case management agency follow up on referral services regarding her recently diagnosed scoliosis and ensure that recommendations are addressed, and intervention is immediate.

8. It is recommended that the full case management agency investigate additional relative placements and other prospective caregivers and home studies conducted to determine the appropriateness of those placements as placement options.

It's ironic that a few of the recommendations stemmed from information reported in the 2005 and 2006 investigation reports that were closed with no indicators, a clear indication that somebody had dropped the ball.

For instance, I was referred to His House Children's Home to receive ongoing case management services, but I was never assigned a guardian ad litem.[2] The doctor had diagnosed me with scoliosis, and I had undergone several x-rays; however, I never completed the treatment plan. Additionally, I had been referred to Kristi House for an unknown service. Kristi House is known for treating sexually abused children. However, I do not recall going there. There is a record on file that indicates someone from the agency signed a confidentiality log on 8/22/2008 at 2:30 p.m. and signed out at 2:50 p.m. I do not know the context of that meeting.

I was referred to Our Kids Our Future to undergo a psychological evaluation. The case manager requested expedited services. The agency replied to inform the case manager that two appointments had been scheduled. I was scheduled to be seen on 10/9/2008 to complete an intake and again on 10/28/2008 to be evaluated by the psychiatrist.

I attended all my appointments, and the therapist summarized the recommendations:

Reason for Referral: Kenisha Anthony is a seventeen-year-old African American female who was referred by a His House Children's Home case manager for a mental health assessment that included a psychiatric evaluation and recommendations regarding ongoing mental health treatment. She has an unfortunate background history of multiple family and non-family placements after termination of parental rights from her mother's care as a younger child. She has no formal prior psychiatric diagnosis or any significant prior mental health treatment.

The psychiatrist recommended (1) At this point, I do not see any psychiatric condition that would justify medication treatment (2) I do think Kenisha could benefit from supportive psychotherapy interventions, although she seems very closed to that idea and certainly would not benefit if she were coerced into taking

---

2   **39.820(1)** — a certified volunteer, a staff attorney, contract attorney, or pro bono attorney working on behalf of a guardian ad litem or the program; appointed by the court to represent the best interests of a child and serves until discharged by the court.

part. If she were open to the idea, I would recommend participation in a trial of supportive individual psychotherapy to address issues of survivorship, self-esteem, improved trust, etc. (3) I certainly agree with the other recommendations in the level of care assessment that included an independent living program.

He was right. Even with all my bottled-up emotions, I had chosen not to participate in therapeutic services. I wasn't educated about the benefits of therapy or how to properly treat traumatic experiences. I thought whatever happened had happened, and I couldn't change it. I didn't see the benefits of speaking to a therapist. It would have been just my luck to open up to yet another person and be called a liar. It wasn't worth the risk. I wasn't ready to deal with the trauma. I didn't have the time or mental space. Plus, I was in a new home. This was a chance for a fresh start.

It wasn't the best decision, but I don't regret denying services. Had I done so, everything discussed in therapy would have been inputted into a status report submitted to the courts, including further recommendations. And who knows what can of worms that would have opened.

But you will not see the light until you have faced what's in the dark. Pain weighs you down and shows up in your life in unexpected ways. Carrying pain is not easy. People warned me, "You'll have a mental breakdown if you don't let go of what's hurting you." I've spent many years being cold, numb, and distant. I don't become attached to people. It's easy for me to cut people off and never speak to them again. For some time, I subconsciously failed to extend hugs. An old friend of mine fought to teach me how to greet her with a hug. I'd just say, "What's up" when we met. I don't like to be touched or have people invading too much of my personal space. I find peace in being a loner.

Court orders and custody had been sorted out. I was successfully enrolled into Miami Edison Senior High, which I attended that upcoming school year. But because I had missed the second quarter of the last school year, I had to repeat the tenth grade. After moving away from with Jasmine to live with Gina, Jasmine withdrew me from Carol City Senior High. Because my family was too busy trying to encourage me to get a GED, I had attended

Dorsey Educational Center instead of transferring to regular public school while living with Gina. Dorsey's curriculum was different than that of a regular school.

At Miami Edison, I spoke with the school counselor to see if there was any chance of me getting into my proper grade, but the option included a heavy course load, so I opted to repeat tenth grade and attend night school, making up classes I had failed during freshman year to catch up.

Back at home, things were good for a while. It had been a long time since someone had shown any form of affection toward me. It had been an even longer time since I'd used the word "mom." It felt good calling out, "Maaaaaaa!" Sometimes, I said it just because I could.

There was an instance when my teacher thought she could kick me out of class because she didn't approve of the fit of my uniform. Brooke came to the school to address the issue with the principal. She was appalled that after the money she'd spent on my uniforms, the teacher was preventing me from getting my education. By the end of the conversation, the teacher was instructed to admit me back into her class.

Even though things were good at home, sometimes forgetting my reality was nearly impossible. When Brooke came to my school, other students blatantly questioned me about calling her mom because she was light-skinned and I'm dark-skinned. I responded by adamantly confirming that she was my mother without any further explanation, not that it was any of their business, anyhow. But convincing them was impossible. They reiterated, "That is not your mama," highlighting the fact that I didn't look like either her or her daughter.

To occupy myself, I decided to try out for the marching Red Raiders flagette squad, and I made the team. I found joy in performing at the weekly football games. Brooke attended and sat alongside the band to watch the performance. But there was one issue—we didn't have the money to pay for my uniform. I was embarrassed to tell my peers I couldn't remain on the squad because I couldn't afford the uniform. I stalled and made excuses until the excuses got old and I quit. When I finally told the truth, my teammates were surprised and said they thought I had it made. I hadn't the slightest clue as to what gave them that impression, but I guess it was how I carried myself.

The system wasn't going to pay expenses for extracurricular activities. My case manager said no to almost everything, even buying a phone charger. Sometimes, I lucked up and got a ten-dollar Wal-Mart gift card, which I used to buy hygiene products, but that was rare. And maybe there was some truth to Brooke's not being able to afford a uniform that cost more than $1,000, but as a child, I had a different perspective.

Children undoubtedly take mental notes about what's happening around them. They notice everything. It was simple to notice the difference in the things Brooke did for herself and biological daughter opposed to what she did for me.

There wasn't a time when her hair or her daughter's hair was undone. Getting their hair done was law. They got new styles nearly every two weeks. Her daughter had the opportunity to participate in optimist cheerleading, a cheerleading league for kids. She never had to abruptly quit the squad or stop participating because of finances or any other reason. Even if she complained, Brooke always made a way. If her daughter was acting out and Brooke threatened to make her quit, she always went back on her word.

I never went with them to any of the competitions. I only cared to celebrate the major holidays: birthdays, the Fourth of July, Thanksgiving, and Christmas. Where I'm from, it was customary to get fresh for the holidays with a fly new outfit, a new pair of kicks, a fresh hairstyle and set of nails. It was the culture. But I had become accustomed to going without, even when others had.

On Thanksgiving Day, I came downstairs to get a plate of food and went back to my room. I heard the whispers about how I was always isolating myself. On Christmas Day, I watched Brooke's daughter open gifts and wondered why Brooke couldn't sacrifice at least the tree to get me one. Her daughter even got gifts from her grandmother. I saw them buy her the same portable TV every year. And every year, she broke it. Later in the evening, when all my friends flaunted their fly looks, I'd put on a hat or hoodie to cover my undone hair and throw on something from the closet so I could still hang out.

While living with Brooke, I dealt with a lot of uncertainty. One minute, it felt like I had nothing to worry about, but at other times, she reminded me to never get too comfortable. It seemed every time I began letting my guard down, things changed.

When I thought I was a lesbian and explored a childish relationship with another girl, to protect her daughter from my homosexual influence, Brooke threatened to kick me out of her house. But when she received her income tax return, she gave me money—a one-time thing. She once gifted me a G-Shock watch as a birthday present. It was my favorite color, purple. And on another occasion, she bought me a cell phone, but it was my responsibility to pay the monthly bill, which wasn't a rational deal. It was no secret that I didn't have an income. Plus, she ensured that her biological child's bill was paid. I was irresponsible and shouldn't have accepted the phone, but I wanted one. What was a teenager without a cell phone? Everyone had one.

To earn money, I started doing individual rope twist extensions, charging $150 per head. With minimal clientele, doing hair kept a few dollars in my pocket. The downside was that I hated the amount of time styling consumed. I started to feel nauseous by the time I got to the middle section of a client's head, but I needed the money. To participant in band activities, I used the money to buy practice clothes and a uniform set before it was time to purchase the squad's real uniforms.

My efforts went unnoticed.

My behavior had declined. I had started skipping class again and acting out in school. Between my behavior, Brooke's uncertainty about who she wanted me to be, and both our emotions, there was friction. I decided to go to McDonald's one morning before school started, and I arrived at school after the school bell rang. I was only a few minutes late, but school officials locked me out. I knew what was going to happen. I begged the principal not to call her, but he said he didn't have a choice. He sentenced me to indoor suspension, and I was kicked out of Brooke's house.

Brooke told the principal to contact my case manager to let him know I was no longer welcome at her house. He picked me up from school and advised that we would get my belongings on a later date. My placement status changed to licensed care, which means I was placed in a home that was licensed by the State to care for foster kids. I moved into His House Children's Home. The only cottage with bed space was designed for toddlers. As a teenager, I settled in with colorful walls, cartoons, teddy bears, toys, and active kids. The house mom resembled the comedic Tyler Perry character Madea and had an attitude like Miss Trunchbull, the tyrannical headmistress from *Matilda*. She appeared to be withdrawn and allowed the staff to tend to the children.

Before I could settle into the house, the staff were required to educate me about the house rules, and I had to complete paperwork that required my signature. I don't remember what all the documents were about. But I do know one of them was to document all the things I'd come with.

After getting my signature, the staff woman showed me around to familiarize me with the house. She showed me where I would sleep, my designated storage space, and other parts of the house. The refrigerator and cabinets were secured with padlocks, preventing us from eating at our own convenience. The staff supplied me with a hygiene kit, including a toothbrush for the teeth of a toddler, children's toothpaste, deodorant, and soap. Because I had come with only the clothes on my back, the staff took me to a shed to shuffle through used garments. During the tour, I kept silent and took mental notes that would be released through tears and a sleepless night. While crying, a bright light flashed in my face. It was the midnight shift conducting bed checks to ensure none of the children were missing.

The staff woke everyone up in the morning to get dressed for school. I used the kiddy toothbrush and toothpaste, put on the old hand-me-down uniform, and ate cereal for breakfast. A big white van dropped me off at school. Thankfully, I was the last drop off, so none of the other kids were on the bus. Plus, I was late, so the other students didn't see me when I arrived.

It was the first day of the Florida Comprehension Assessment Test.

The FCAT determined if a student would earn a high school diploma. I had witnessed other students fail and become ineligible for graduation. I was nervous about not graduating from high school. I hadn't the slightest idea about what I could do with myself without a high school diploma.

I walked into class late, sat at my desk, and bit into an apple. The house parent hadn't let me get a second bowl of cereal and gave me an apple to go. After two bites, I felt my emotions begin to boil. Before receiving any of the testing materials, tears burst from my eyes, and I ran out of class in an uproar. I crashed onto the bathroom floor, distraught about my situation.

"Get me out of that place!" I screamed as my home economics teacher tried to comfort me, making me regret each time I had disrespected her.

I didn't take the test that day. However, I took it later, passing only the reading portion.

My needs continued to go unmet. My hair was styled in a sleek pretzel ponytail, which was meant to last about two weeks. I had come into licensed care with the style, and with already a week's worth of wear and excessive scratching, giving it a fuzzy, worn look, it was time for it to come out of my head. I needed my hair done, a perm, and a new style. I continuously let the staff know that I needed my hair done. And on numerous occasions, they reassured me that it would get done but never said when. Time passed and frustration grew as my hair looked a total mess. Every day in school, I wore a jacket with a hoodie to cover my hair. My teachers nagged me about it, instructing me to take the hoodie off, but I had no other choice but to disobey them, causing myself more trouble.

I suffered through another week with unkempt hair, what felt like a massive headache, lack of sleep, and a load of stress. I needed a break to think, so I ran away instead of waiting for the bus to pick me up from school. While on the run, I was able to get my belongings and get my hair done. I called Brooke and asked if I could pick up my belongings. And I asked one of Jasmine's god-sisters to do my hair. They both agreed, and I found rides to meet them. To avoid worrying about my hair for a few months, I got it styled into plaits. Some may say it's just hair, but not to me. I like to look nice and clean. To me, hair is a determining factor for self-esteem. I feel messy, ugly, and unorganized when my hair isn't done. And people won't forget to confirm those sentiments.

Eventually, built-up frustration about my unkempt hair led me to the nearest barbershop. I cut it all off to a low boy cut. I felt lighter, like I had one less life problem to worry about. Managing the baldhead jokes wasn't an issue.

In the meantime, I stayed with friends, contemplating about life and my next move. After some time and some thinking, I came to a middle ground with myself. I'd accept living in the group home, aging out, and move on with my life. But my plan failed. I couldn't return to the house where I'd mentally prepared to live, because I had run away. When I returned, I waited at the front door, and a staff member handed me my belongings. She noticed I had a new hairstyle and brought it to the attention of the others.

She said, "Kenisha, you didn't have to run away; we were going to get your hair done."

I didn't feel the need to respond.

I moved to a new placement, a group home designated for teenagers. The same rules applied; I had to complete an inventory check, sign paperwork, and be advised of the rules before settling in. There were many rules. Padlocks covered the cabinets and fridge, and there were timed showers and a set bedtime. I had promised my friend Shakira I would call to let her know I was okay, but kids were prohibited from using the house phone with no exceptions. It was a safety issue. I spoke with my case manager about getting a personal cell phone. Having a phone required a court order, and I would be responsible for paying the monthly bill. I didn't have money. Hair clients weren't allowed at the house, and getting approval to travel to them would've been a headache, so I avoided it altogether. Who would get fingerprinted and allow the system to invade their life and home just to get their hair done?

Normalcy was non-existent. I couldn't bear to live under those conditions. They prevented me from taking care of myself. If I was still going to be responsible for meeting my own needs, I preferred to at least live in a home with less restrictions. Weighing my options, I told my case manager about Ivy's mother and provided him her contact information, thinking hopefully I could move with her. He claimed after a few attempts he couldn't make contact with her. My first choice didn't work out so, I resorted to my second option. I told my case manager to ask Brooke if I could return to her home. She said yes. A court hearing was scheduled, and the judge granted a modification of placement. My placement status changed back to non-relative care.

In less than six months, I would turn eighteen years old. I figured I'd tough it out and stay out of the way. If I was invisible, I wouldn't be a burden. I stayed in my room to avoid conflict. It didn't work. Brooke still complained, reminding me that no one cared, and once I turned eighteen, I would be on my own.

"You'll be grown," she'd say. I didn't know why she was always telling me that. But I soon found out that she was calling and complaining to Ashley, Jasmine, Grandma Rose, and people I thought were my friends, fake friends who talked about me behind my back and made fun of me for being a foster kid and caused much of the trouble I got into at school.

I was easily triggered when people mentioned anything about my situation. I guess because my family didn't come take me off her hands, Brooke felt they didn't care. I repeatedly told my case manager I wanted to leave, which he noted in his home visit notes, but he always recommended that I stay.

CHAPTER SEVEN

Aged Out

"Sometimes, you have to bank on yourself, believe in your ideas and fight for it despite what people think."
- Queen Latifah

"More than 23,000 children age out of the foster care system each year. Most are without emotional and financial support and are at high risk of becoming homeless, having poor educational achievement, and involvement in the criminal justice system."
- NFYI

Time was limited. My eighteenth birthday was approaching quickly. The upcoming court hearing was the last before being released from supervision of the State and officially aging out. Court always went by so fast. I barely ever got a word in or understood what the hearing was about. All I knew was that it was about me being in foster care. I couldn't allow that to happen at this hearing; I had to speak up. I prepped myself to explain to the judge that I was not in a stable home, and the plan to achieve permanency[1] was not at all permanent. My guardian and I didn't have a positive, healthy, and nurturing relationship. She hadn't even accompanied me at the court hearing. I wanted to express that with the benefits of the Independent Living Program, I could fund the foundation of my adult life. As a participant of the Independent Living Program, I would've been guaranteed a $1,300 check every month until age 23 and assistance with getting my own place to live. The money would have gone toward my basic needs and bus fare to travel to and from school.

---

1 **Permanency** — having positive, healthy, nurturing relationships with adults who provide emotional, financial, moral, educational, and other kinds of support as youth mature into adults.

I tried.

But on the day of the hearing, the judge said there was nothing more the system could do since my eighteenth birthday was near. The issue was that I was in non-relative care and had not spent at least six months in a licensed placement, which didn't meet the criteria to receive independent living services.

My case manager advocated for me, stating that he had witnessed judges order children into licensed care a day before their eighteen birthdays so they could be enrolled into the program due to their circumstances. However, my judge didn't agree and refused to make the exception for me.

Reviewing my file, it noted that it was unknown if I'd spent any time in licensed care. If I had, it was before 2003. That's a clear indication that somewhere along the way, someone had dropped the ball. Based on that information, the judge could have questioned, "Where has this child been?" and "Who has molded this child to be ready for adulthood?" He then could've made an informed decision based on the professionals' responses. But it didn't happen that way.

I didn't understand the system. I'd been a dependent of the state of Florida since I was four years old. I was never reunified with either my mother or father. According to the system's methodology, I was removed and ordered into the care of people who had turned out to be unreliable and had received years of poor supervision. The system is supposed to remove children from their troubled parents to prevent them from experiencing further trauma, but what good had it done for me? All I ever heard was what the system couldn't do for me in my time of need.

Fed up, I stormed out of the courtroom with built-up frustration and the intent to never look back. I was tired of asking to be cared for, loved, protected, and guided. I was tired of being told no. There was nothing anyone could ever do for me.

Adulthood was rapidly approaching. I wasn't ready, but I knew I had to pull myself up by the bootstraps. All I had was me. In the eyes of the law, I was grown. I had no choice but to do what was best for me with zero excuses. The fate of my future was in my own hands now. First things first—I needed to graduate high school. I was in the eleventh grade and still had one year and some months to go.

I don't remember how long it was, but before my case came to a close, my case manager changed again. Still trying to understand why the system couldn't do anything for me, I advised the new case manager that my previous case manager had provided the wrong information about eligibility requirements to receive independent living services. The new case manager consulted with her supervisor about the issue, but there was nothing more she could do. Time was up. Generously, the last thing she gave me was another ten-dollar gift card.

What level of permanency was I guaranteed? The independent living plan in my foster care record is blank, so I know there was never really a plan. I was living with someone familiar, which was a good thing, but it came with a cost. My caregiver had a family of her own to care for—her words. She only provided basic shelter needs, always complained, threatened to kick me out, and didn't think I was her responsibility after I turned eighteen. The tension stemmed from financial burdens to care for me, expenses she expected the State to cover. And when the State said no, it cost me a stable place to live and created further emotional and mental anguish.

The State did their job, taking my picture every month to document that I was alive and hosted pointless court hearings to discuss my well-being but not my future. They dictated what I could and couldn't do based on the rules and provided health insurance until I turned eighteen. It seems both Brooke and the State pacified the situation until they could no longer be implicated as responsible parties if something bad happened. It felt like they were watching the clock, anxious for October 7, my birthday, so they could say, "You're an adult."

My upbringing was guarded by bureaucracy with no permanent plan for adulthood. Everyone voiced their opinion, nitpicked, and chose what they were willing to contribute due to my parents' absence. But at eighteen, I would be left to fend for myself with little to no money and no guidance or safety net if I fell short. I would be on my own without the leverage of being a child or support from those I expected to care about me.

Even though I was ineligible to receive financial benefits, I attended a few independent living classes. The instructor taught life skills such as writing checks, budgeting, and paying bills. To participate, I had to travel about two hours on the bus from Miami Shores to Miami Gardens, sacrificing money I didn't have for bus fare. I spoke with the independent living coordinator of His House Children's Home. Her response was the same as the others: there was nothing more to be done in my case. I inquired about other programs that could possibly help, but she claimed to not have knowledge of any programs that would be useful to my situation. She advised that I was eligible to attend college with tuition exemption.[2] It was good information to know, but not what I needed at the time. I didn't have the mental capacity to think about college or budgeting. I was broke, hungry, and on the verge of homelessness, and I needed to finish high school. Eventually, I stopped going to the class.

What is the difference between a child aging out of licensed care and a child aging out of non-relative care if they both lack a strong support system post eighteen? Youth who have a case plan goal of APPLA, whether their placement is licensed or not, should be eligible to receive independent living services. At the least, it's something to rely on. It only makes sense. If the placement is secure, the Department should explore case plan goals other than APPLA and close the case before the child turns eighteen. Why not adoption? In my case, a non-relative was approved as a placement option but denied licensing, leaving me with little to no resources and a slim chance of becoming a self-sufficient adult.

Everyone's level of resilience is different. I think about youth that were in the same position as myself at eighteen. I know it can be tough, and I know where it can lead: jail, homelessness, drug use, or suicide. I wonder how their lives turned out and can only hope they overcame the struggle.

---

2   **s. 1009.25(1)(d)** — The following students are exempt from the payment of tuition and fees, including lab fees, at a school district that provides postsecondary career programs, Florida College System institution, or state university: (d) A student who is or was at the time he or she reached 18 years of age in the custody of a relative under s. 39.5085 or who was adopted from the Department of Children and Family Services after May 5, 1997. Such exemption includes fees associated with enrollment in career-preparatory instruction. The exemption remains valid until the student reaches 28 years of age.

State of Florida
Department of Children and Families

Rick Scott
Governor

David E. Wilkins
Secretary

Date: June 13, 2011

To: Florida Public State University, Public Florida College System Institution, or
Public Postsecondary Career and Technical Program

From: _____, Department of Children and Families
or Community Based Care Lead Agency

Title: INDEPENDENT LIVING COORIDNATOR

Subject: Tuition and Fee Exemption for Students Receiving or Formerly Receiving Services from the
Department of Children and Families

Please accept this letter certifying that _____ KENISHA ANTHONY _____ (name),
whose date of birth is ___October 7, 1991___, meets one of the following criteria necessary to obtain
exemption from paying tuition and fees at a **Florida public** state university, **public** Florida College System
institution or **public** postsecondary career and technical program, pursuant to the "Florida K-20 Education
Code," Section 1009.25(2)(c)-(d), Florida Statutes (check one):

☑ He or she is or was at the time he or she reached age 18 in the custody of the Department of
Children and Families;

☐ He or she was adopted from the Department of Children and Families after May 5, 1997;

☐ He or she is or was at the time of reaching age 18 in the custody of a relative under s. 39.5085, F.S.;
or,

☐ He or she was placed in a guardianship by the court after reaching age 16 and spending at least 6
months in the custody of the Department of Children and Families.

The tuition and fee exemption **CANNOT** be used at an out-of-state educational institution or in-state private
university, private community college or private postsecondary career and technical program. Please contact
the financial aid office at the school to determine whether alternative tuition and fee exemptions or
scholarships are available through the school.

**Effective July 1, 2010[1], this exemption remains valid until the young person reaches the age 28, which
is ___October 7, 2020___.**

Please contact _____, Florida Department of Children and Families
or Community Based Care Agency at _____ for additional information.

_____
School Official, if applicable

_____
School Official, if applicable

_____
[1] Please note: If you are receiving this form when leaving the custody of DCF, but are not ready to use the exemption at this time,
you will need to read Section 1009.25(2)(c), F.S., to ensure that the statute still provides the tuition and fee exemption for former
foster youth in the category in which you qualify. Florida laws may change from year to year.

CF-FSP 5220, PDF 02/2011

CHAPTER EIGHT

Adulthood

*"You may not control all the events that happen to you, but you can
decide not to be reduced by them."*
- Dr. Maya Angelou

After the drama with the system, I continued living with Brooke. Again, I figured I'd stay out of her way and make a way for myself to keep tension down. After submitting tons of applications, attending on-the-spot job interviews, and never getting calls back, I finally got a summer job through a workforce program the summer before my twelfth grade year. The program was designated for teenagers and young adults. Applicants were selected in a lottery pick. Luckily, I was chosen. The position was only for six weeks, which allowed me to earn three paychecks. It was just what I needed to buy back-to-school and hygiene necessities and, of course, get my hair and nails done. It also covered the cost of breakfast, lunch, and bus fare to and from work. I was dedicated to keeping the job; excuses were unacceptable.

Since money was an issue for Brooke, I thought I was eliminating the problem, even if it was only for the moment. But it still wasn't good enough. Her mind was made up. She wanted me out of her house, and she only needed to tell me one more time.

I left and went to a friend's house until I figured out what I was going to do next. But I couldn't stay forever. It had been a few years since I had spoken to Ashley. I was still upset about what had happened when I lived with her previously, but, still, I picked up the phone and called her. I was out of options.

"Can I live with you again?" I asked.

She said yes. She was no longer with her old boyfriend who had sexually assaulted me. I called Jasmine for a ride. She picked me up from my friend's house to take me to get my packed belongings and dropped me off at Ashley's house. Brooke wasn't home. I placed her key on the counter, sent her a text message to let her know, and left. I left without my birth certificate and social security card. According to Brooke, she could not find either of them.

I became fully aware of Brooke's issues after I'd left. For some reason, she was under the impression that I wasn't serious about graduating, on the verge of dropping out, and was a paymaster, spending all my money on friends and boys versus contributing to the household, specifically cleaning supplies. It was never my responsibility to buy cleaning supplies. She'd told everyone but me these things. And she was only telling half the truth, which made it an entire lie.

Yes, I did spend a few dollars on my friends now and then—and I mean just that—a few, like buying food from McDonald's or Wing Stop. When I didn't have money, they'd used money their parents had given them to buy me stuff so I wouldn't be left out. While driving their parents' cars, I was the only friend who didn't contribute to gas because I didn't have money. So, when I could, I returned the favor.

I remember Brooke having a conversation with me, but it didn't include any of those concerns. She only told me that due to my being withdrawn and secluded, she thought it was best that I return to my biological family.

It confused me that a person would be upset about expectations they had never set. A parent would have a conversation with her child. Then again, I wasn't her child; I only wanted to be. Before I secured a temporary income, there were things I wanted and needed, things she didn't buy me, so I tended to my own needs when I earned a little cash. I wouldn't change my actions if I could turn back the hands of time. I had to take care of myself since it was an issue for everyone else.

I've learned that people will never treat foster children like their own children because they're not. Maybe it's impossible to do so because they don't share a biological connection. The child is only a person to whom they're extending help until they get tired of doing so. Reviewing my foster care record, I saw that it was documented in a home visit note that Brooke had told my case manager if they didn't give her any financial assistance, I would have to be removed from her home. It stated that I was sad during the visit because she couldn't afford to buy me a dress to wear for Christmas. She highlighted that she had a family of her own to care for. The report was right; I felt like an outcast because I was an outcast. Was I not a member of the family? I remember the case manager recommending that she become licensed to get money. She had tried but failed due to a history of domestic violence, although she was the victim.

It all boiled down to the underlying problem: I wanted a mother. I wanted a father. I wanted my mother and father. I just wanted to be a child for once. I wanted to be protected. I wanted to be loved and cared for. I wanted to love myself, but my environment prevented me from doing so. I had watched the adults around me care for themselves and love their children. I had observed children being dependent on their parents. But whenever those adults had to do the same for me, it was an issue. I needed to grow up fast to fend for myself—with no knowledge or guidance on how to do that.

"We were raised wrong, but we stayed strong."
– **Nipsey Hussle**

Trouble is easy to get into and hard to get out of. The saying is cliché because people tend to think one's actions are the cause of their troubles when that may not be the case.

What I consider a simple high school fight led to my stay in the slammer as an adult. My friend, Shakira and I had jumped another student named Crystal. But the fight had started by no fault of our own. She had started with us. We'd had a few run-ins with her crew throughout the school year, so this incident only added more fuel to the fire.

It was lunch time, and Shakira and I were standing in line getting our food. The girl had to have awakened that morning with fighting on her mind because she opened the lunch door, looked at us, and said, "I'm going to beat this bitch ass today."

Confused as to which one of us she was talking to, Shakira and I went outside to the patio and confronted her. Shakira did the talking, but Crystal never confirmed who she was talking to. She was busy making a complete fool of herself. Her shoes were off, and she was screaming at the top of her lungs while on the phone with her mother. She was just showing off and making a pointless scene.

I had wasted my money because I didn't even get to eat my lunch. Crystal took the first swing. Before I knew it, we were in a brawl. I always blacked out when I fought. Next thing I knew, I was on top of a security guard's shoulder being carried away and the principal was hauling Crystal away. Misguidedly, they took us through the same double doors, so I took a few more punches at her. Shakira and I were later arrested while Crystal went free. It wasn't fair. I wanted to press charges against her as well; she had assaulted me, but authorities ignored that fact. I think the school authorities were sick of me, anyhow, and used the fight as a way to kick me out of their school.

I had caught my second criminal case. I was charged with aggravated assault with bodily harm, disruption of an educational setting, and resisting arrest without violence. Trying to avoid the big house, I gave the police officer a false birthday. I changed my birth year to the date of a minor, but, of course, it didn't work. The officer kept asking questions because she couldn't locate me in the system. I was eighteen years old. Shakira was still underage, so they put her in a separate car. She went to juvenile detention, and I was hauled off to the Miami-Dade County Jail.

As the patrol car entered the concrete gate topped with barbed wire, I felt my freedom being stripped away in a matter of seconds. As I underwent the booking process, I felt degraded. I felt pure humiliation as I was forced to get naked and expose my sacred jewels, bending over and coughing during my first strip search.

It was just my luck; I ran into Jasmine's girlfriend and her godmother's sister. We were all in the same cell. In a room full of people, our conversations weren't private.

I read my A-form aloud, and everyone in the cell chimed in with their thoughts.

"Oh, this is your first time. You'll get out."

"You're young, and it was just a school fight. You'll get out."

"You'll get out on pre-trial release."

Their amateur philosophies put me at ease because this wasn't their first rodeo.

They were all wrong. I learned to never listen to jailhouse lawyers; they don't know what they're talking about. If they knew the law, they wouldn't have been inmates next to me.

My name was called through a small square window built into the steel door. It was somebody from the pre-trial department collecting my information. Everybody reiterated what they'd already predicted, hyping me up. "See, I told you; you'll be out in the morning."

All I had to do was survive one night in the county jail. I sat on the hard, cracked floor, waiting for the bus to the women's annex to arrive and take me to the next destination. The night started out uncomfortably. It took a long time for the bus to the women's jail to come. When it finally did, I had to be strip-searched again to transition into the jail. I asked why I had to go through that again, and an officer explained that it was because of my charges. I was labeled aggressive.

I hardly got any sleep. The cot was hard, the sheets were thin, the pillow didn't have any fluff, and the lights stayed on all night. The worst part was that it was time to wake up the moment my eyes had closed.

Court hearings never start on time, and the wait time is always ridiculous. I was grouchy. I had been up since 4 a.m. only to be denied pre-trial release and given $10,000 bail. I was in disbelief. Crystal appeared in court wearing a neck brace. She must have forgotten she'd started the fight. Although I hadn't asked, Brooke enlightened my family about my incarceration. No one had the money to bond me out. I wasn't surprised, nor did I expect them to help me. I don't even know why she called them. I did what I do best—adapted to the environment and did my time.

During the first few moments back in the holding cell, I told myself I would never come back to this place. One of the inmates was bleeding. Her menstrual cycle had come on, and she didn't have any sanitary products. Other inmates tried to help, signaling the correctional officers by screaming and banging on the steel doors, but they were ignored. My stomach was in a ball.

I spent most of the time asleep. I only woke up for headcount, lawyer visits, food trays, timed showers, and to be transferred to other jails. The food was disgusting. We were served either bologna or salami sandwiches. Unfortunately, the officers always managed to give me salami and wouldn't allow me to switch. The salami had black spots, the spaghetti was awful, and the juice tasted like medicine. I held my nose to swallow the stuff. I eventually stopped forcing myself to eat the food and resorted to surviving off bread and water until I was released.

Weeks passed, and I hadn't heard anything about getting out. My first cellmate made the time seem dreadful. She kept a calendar to X out every day she'd completed in lock up. That damn near drove me crazy, but she was cool. She always woke me up and told me what I needed to do when the correctional officers came into the cell. I remember one of them flashing a light in my face while I was asleep. It reminded me of being back in the group home. For no reason, I got moved to another cell. My new cellmate appeared to be a lesbian, a stud. I prayed the rumors about getting raped in jail weren't true.

I lost sight of the outside. I rarely called home because I didn't want to be a burden. Being an inmate can be costly. I didn't ask for commissary because I didn't want to hear "no," and I refused to complete a visitation list to avoid the disappointment of no one coming to see me.

While asleep, I jumped up because my name was being called on the loud speaker. It turned out to be a visit from a public defender. I signed the papers for her to represent me, and we talked about the case and the upcoming court hearing. I had been in jail for about two months. Although I was released at the next hearing, the court case wasn't over. I still had to report to court, and the "victim" continued to show up. For a while, the hearings were repeatedly rescheduled, which was a waste of my day and the bus fare it took to travel downtown.

I didn't understand where this case was headed. And, to scare me, the judge said things like, "You're facing up to ten years in prison." The security guard that had broken up the fight appeared at one of the hearings. I knew, for sure, he would be on my side. Wrong. He testified against me. The case continued to drag until Crystal stopped showing up. The prosecutor finally gave the case up, and my record was marked with no action and nolle pros, which meant some charges were dropped and others would no longer be pursued.

I had a run-in with the arresting officer. Because of my distaste for her and her decision to arrest me, I wasn't interested in having a conversation with her, although she still managed to let me know that she'd arrested me to teach me a lesson, one I have yet to discover. The only thing I've gained from that situation is the need to explain the aggressive charges anytime a background screening is required.

"God put rainbows in the clouds so that each of us—in the dreariest and most dreaded moments—can see a possibility of hope."
– **Dr. Maya Angelou**

I was released from jail, but my life underwent yet another transition. I had been expelled from Miami Edison. I needed a new school, and with my history, that wouldn't be easy. No schools were waiting to welcome me with open arms. Brooke and I visited several schools, including an alternative school, but none of them were willing to take a chance. During interviews, they discussed the number of behavior referrals I'd received, my poor attendance record, and my age. They also mentioned that I had an insufficient number of course credits. My last hope was attending Miami Central Senior High. Thank God they accepted me.

This was my fourth high school and last chance. I had to do it right. I'll admit, I wasn't perfect. We could all use a few more chances before we get it all the way right. I continued to skip classes, but I didn't cause any trouble, meaning I didn't get into any fights to disrupt school. I had two fights, but I waited until we were off school grounds. I was trying.

I was dedicated to Junior Reserves Officers' Training Corps (JROTC). I earned higher ranks and made sure my uniforms were creased and my hair never touched my collar. I didn't attend the annual ball for financial reasons. The plan was for the military to be my escape route from my problems. I could get away, have a steady income, and see the world. I even joined the drill team to keep myself occupied. It was the one activity I didn't have to quit because uniforms and participation were free.

But trouble had its way of finding me.

I had been having some trouble with one of the girls at school but did my best to avoid a physical altercation. But sometimes, I just had to do what I had to do.

Following my daily after-school routine, I was getting ready to start drill team practice when I received a phone call. A friend told me the girl was ready to fight. Fed up, I provided a location and told them to meet me there. I left practice, and it went down from there. The videos of the fight are on YouTube: *Brownsub Hampton House Vol. 1* and *Vol. pt 2*. I have tried to report the videos for removal, but YouTube has yet to honor my request.

Home economics was my second favorite course. I consistently attended and participated in class. At the end of senior year, I earned a culinary certificate for mastering all the levels. I don't know where the certificate is now. The class setting was small and intimate, and my classmates and I got along pretty well.

One day, my classmate, Lorne, noticed my rare last name, Anthony, and asked if I had a sister named Mylika. It just so happened that I did. She was my paternal sister. Shockingly, Lorne was my sister's brother on her mom's side. At a point in my life, I hadn't even known I had a little sister, but once I found out, I remember only seeing her once. After that, I hadn't seen her in years. Just like that, we were reconnected. Our next moment together was spent watching Mylika off to her eighth-grade prom.

As adults, we've had the opportunity to talk about being apart for so long. As kids, we didn't see each other often. We reminisced about the one and only time I had gone to her house. We were dressed like twins and played with toys. The conversation led to me asking her why her mother never tried to come get me. Mylika explained that her mother was present in court when the judge decided to remove me from my parents' custody. She said, "The judge asked my mom if she would care for you, but because she had two kids of her own and she was pregnant with me at the time, she wasn't able."

She also managed to bring me to tears with another story. One time, her mom had brought me Christmas presents, and she claimed to have tried to deliver them to me, but Shawn didn't allow it because there were no gifts for her children. Hearing about people and their spiteful ways made me angry all over again, but it brought me comfort to know her mom had thought about me.

"She'd have random thoughts like, "I wonder what Kenisha is doing," Mylika said.

I'm happy to be reconnected with my sister. I like to call her "little big sister." I'm still a little rough around the edges, and she's the cool, calm, and collected one. I think we're the perfect balance. Now that we're adults, I'll never let anything else keep us apart. Over the last few years, we've built a bond and continue to grow closer.

"Hard days are the best because that's when champions are made."
— **Gabby Douglas**

"About one in four children that age out of foster care will not graduate from high school or be able to pass the GED test."
— **NFYI**

Out of other options, I focused on graduating from high school. And to do so, I had a lot of catching up to do. I was a senior and didn't have all my credits. Skipping and failing classes had caught up to me. I was already a year behind, so to graduate in 2011, I had to attend day school, virtual school, and night school. My days were long. My weekly schedule, Monday through Thursday, started at 5 a.m. and ended at 11 p.m. Friday was my favorite day of the week. My schedule took a great deal of discipline to execute, but I was determined.

After the first session of night school, I would cry because I was so hungry. I didn't have any money. Sometimes, I would go to a friend's house nearby to eat at least a peanut butter and jelly sandwich before the second session started. Other times, I just dwelled on my situation with an empty stomach. I remember listening to the words of Monica's song "Getaway." I connected with every word. I was overwhelmed with hopeless emotions as tears streamed down my face. Still carrying the burdens of my past and dealing with the situation at hand, it felt like I was never going to catch a break at this thing called life. During those moments, I realized the only option I had was to utilize the tuition exemption waiver to go to college. It was my only hope for a better life, and I had to give every moment after that 110 percent.

I scheduled a meeting with my College Assistance Program advisor to explore college options. She was informative and provided me with the waiver to take the SAT and ACT. For my current classes, I had to earn a passing grade on upcoming assignments and complete any extra credit opportunities. My third-period teacher was giving extra credit for completing college admission applications. I didn't think I would get accepted into a university; however, I still applied because it was beneficial, and the extra credit would help me earn a passing grade.

As I focused on school, Auntie Mae unexpectedly passed away. She'd previously had a stroke, and we had known her days were numbered. Her last words to me were, "I'm fine." She was always so strong. Although I knew she had accepted that death was a part of life and dying meant she'd be home in heaven with her Father, Jesus, I couldn't accept it, and it's still hard today. Even though she couldn't physically care for me, she was always a phone call away. My Auntie Mae was the one person I knew, without a doubt, loved me unconditionally. I wasn't ready to lose her. At her funeral, either Shawn or Jasmine stated that I cried the hardest because I had done Auntie Mae wrong by not coming to Palm Coast before her passing. Disregarding the fact that I was only nineteen years old and grieving, they'd once again found a way to taunt me. But I know Auntie is always with me. Now, she can see everything I do, so I can't disappoint her.

Senior year continued to be emotional and have its ups and downs. For a few weeks, suspicious men were at our school doing their best to be discreet. But it wasn't hard to know who wasn't a regular at Central. I observed them scoping out the entire school. They'd be on the roof and in the hallways carrying metal detector devices. Being from the hood, I just thought, What's going on now? But this time was different.

Shockingly, the men were securing our school for the arrival of President Barack Obama. I was hype, but there was a catch—only selected students could attend the ceremony. I could only hope to be chosen.

The closer we got to the day of Obama's visit, the more secure the school became. The day of the ceremony, Central was secured by secret service agents, barricades, and road detours. Finally, a voice came through the loud speaker, disrupting Spanish class, announcing the names of the students who would get to attend the ceremony. After their names were called, the students had to report to the gym. My friend Shoniece and I held each other's hand in one balled first and crossed our fingers with the other. The voice called students in alphabetical order by last name, so we were up first because both our last names started with the letter A. But it wasn't our lucky day. The voice hadn't called us, and it moved on to the letter B. We shared a moment of disappointment.

I sucked my teeth and said, "Man, I never get picked."

But I had spoken too soon. The voice came back through and called more names. "Kenisha Anthony, Shoniece Adderly . . ."

We were on our way to see Obama! I had intended to get the entry ticket laminated so I could cherish it forever, but, regrettably, it got lost along the way. On the bright side, it was an experience that can never be lost or taken. I added it to my books as a moment of history for me. The energy in the world had shifted for me. I felt my luck had changed.

Being alive to witness a black president and seeing Obama speak in the flesh was a needed breath of fresh air and a taste of hope, but it didn't change reality. Senior activities were approaching. A part of me was kind of hype, or maybe I was just matching the energy of my friends.

Getting back in contact with Mylika was the gateway to reviving a few other relationships. My older sister Joy was around at the time. She is also my paternal sister, who, for much of my life, I didn't know existed. Once I found out about her, I didn't see her for years. She volunteered to pay for me to participate in Grad Bash, a once-in-a-lifetime activity for seniors to celebrate the completion of high school. Together, we attended the meeting to learn about the cost, activities, dates, etc. Unfortunately, I couldn't get in contact with her when it was time to pay the bill. Later, she said she had to pay for a surgical procedure that prevented her from helping me, which was understandable. I wish she had just communicated with me beforehand to avoid the emotional trauma of feeling let down and forgotten again.

In an effort to participate in prom, I went to a local charitable prom dress event. The organization had racks of dresses to choose from. I found a nice olive-green dress that could benefit from alterations. But like everything else, alterations cost money, and everyone claimed they didn't have any money. Wearing the dress as is wasn't an option because of my petite frame. Most clothes required alterations to fit me. Then there would still be the cost of hair, makeup, a manicure, and shoes. Had I opted to go without all the required prom essentials, I would have been the laughing stock of prom. Every year on social media, prom looks were judged, and people did not bite their tongues. They'd attack my picture with their harsh, unneeded opinions.

To relieve myself from further frustration, I settled on not participating in any of the activities. The day of prom, I watched everyone upload prom pictures, memorializing the festivities. I wished I had families like theirs. Every time I watched Love and Basketball, I dreamed of sharing a moment with my mother, accessorizing my look for the night with our historic family jewels before she sent me off to prom.

I paid twenty dollars to purchase a ticket to the senior picnic, but I still didn't attend because I didn't have an outfit. I felt I had wasted the money, but I did get my senior shirt, so at least I had paid for that.

It was fourth quarter, and senior year was near an end. After slaving due to mistakes for which I take full accountability, my commitment to graduate was soon to pay off. I was in good standing in my current classes with passing grades. I successfully completed virtual school and night school classes, and the grades I'd earned were high enough to increase my grade point average and meet graduation requirements. I didn't have the hindrance of the FCAT in my way. I took the test on make-up day and passed the reading section on the first try. After taking a remedial math class, I passed the math portion on the second try. It was now safe to prepare for graduation and receive my high school diploma.

Even in the happiest moments, reality was never too far away. The school had dress code requirements. Under our gowns we could only wear formal white attire, which, of course, I couldn't afford. But God sent an angel. As part of my daily lunch routine, I joined the lunch line and got a milk and chicken sandwich, the same thing I'd eaten every day of senior year, and sat in the same spot at the lunch table. A teacher in the special ed department, who was also a senior activity chaperon, always sat a few seats down from me as she supervised other students. We began to greet each other after seeing each other so frequently and practically eating lunch together. Randomly, one day during lunch, she asked about my lack of participation in senior activities. I was honest in explaining to her my situation. She said she could have helped me had I told her earlier. Well, I didn't know. And after being told no so many times, I was tired of hearing the same ole thing and eventually stopped asking. If I couldn't do it myself, I convinced myself that I didn't need it. Generously, she offered to purchase me a nice white dress and heels to adhere to the graduation dress code. We exchanged contact numbers. I provided her my size, and she kept her word.

Running off minimal sleep and almost too anxious to walk across the stage, on June 6, 2011, I did it. I graduated! I had earned my high school diploma and defined myself. I wasn't a dropout, settling for a GED, or going off to job corps like everyone had suggested. By reaching this goal, I had unlocked my inner strength. If I could take six classes in one day, nine classes in one full term, and pass, I could do anything I put my mind to.

A few of my teachers had always said, "Kenisha's a smart girl. She can do the work; it's her behavior."

I admit, I had skipped classes and gotten into trouble. I'd been suspended and could be aggressive and disrespectful, but not to the extent that everyone had described, which was why I was confused and left to believe they were only finding excuses to exhibit lack of love, affection, and neglect so they could get rid of me. Maybe some people did want to help but didn't want to take sole responsibility for someone else's child, even though they'd signed up to do it. It taught me to always be honest about what I can and can't do because dishonesty and frustration can ultimately cause more harm than good.

"There is no force equal to a woman determined to rise."
– W.E.B Du Bois

It was time to prepare for the next chapter of my life. After receiving denial letters from every university I had applied to—what university would accept a student with a 2.2 GPA?—I took my educational talents to Miami Dade College. It felt good to receive an acceptance letter with my name on it, even from a community college. Everyone was accepted as long as they had a high school diploma. I was just happy the college was giving me an opportunity.

With a background in JROTC, I enrolled into the college ROTC program and chose criminal justice as my major. I didn't go straight to the army, because I would make more money going into the service with a college degree and a background in ROTC. It took a great deal of discipline to keep up with the program. It required physical training three times per week, which meant I had to wake up at four in the morning. Participation was a grade, so I couldn't skip out. Plus, we had physical training tests, which were also a grade. But I did what I needed to do and signed up for early morning classes to compensate my day.

After attending a few class sessions for Introduction to Criminal Justice, I learned I wasn't interested in the field. The topics were dry and boring. And after the second semester of ROTC, I realized I wasn't willing to fight for this country just to escape my problems. There had to be another way.

Running into an issue with financial aid also helped me realize I had a different purpose. When the refund checks dropped, I was confused as to why I hadn't received the full amount. After standing in the long financial aid line, I found out I hadn't submitted my waiver for the spring semester to cover the cost of tuition. I argued that the FAFSA submission was supposed to be once per school year, and I had indicated on the application that I was a ward of the State in addition to submitting the waiver during the fall. It should have been noted for a full school year just as financial aid was awarded. But that wasn't the procedure, and no one had informed me that I had to submit the tuition exemption waiver each semester. The money I was depending on to buy my books, supplies, and monthly bus card, and to care for myself that semester, was gone due to a lack of communication. I was frustrated!

*"I made decisions that I regret, and I took them as learning experiences.
I'm human, not perfect, like anybody else."*
– Queen Latifah

In need of money, I resorted to a new plan. A custodian at the college claimed I could invest $300 into his drug business to earn me more money to hold me over. He appeared to be a cool guy. He hung out with my friends and I on campus. An associate of mine said he was legit, so I took a chance; anything was a risk. I never saw a return on my investment. He claimed his marijuana spot was raided, so I lost my money. I believe he lied and had just robbed me, but there was nothing I could do about it. The drug business wasn't for me. I didn't have any control in that situation, so I resorted to a familiar activity—shoplifting.

A few episodes were sweet; I had gotten away scot-free. I used a buzzer bag to prevent detection by the stores' alarm systems. Other times, I didn't care about buzzing out. But eventually, the practice of shoplifting to earn cash presented a test where I would have to decide whether I wanted to be a college student or criminal.

I was in the mood to treat myself, so I traveled to the mall to steal several pairs of True Religion jeans, which were expensive, so the cost added up quickly. What had been so easy in the past turned into me running through the mall to evade loss prevention as they chased and eventually caught me. Previously, when I was forced to run, I'd gotten away, but not this time. It wouldn't surprise me if this incident was uploaded onto YouTube. People filmed us as we tried to fight off loss prevention workers and get away. I was charged with two felonies, third-degree grand theft, and the use of an antishoplifting device. I found myself contemplating about life in the same jail cell from before, on the same hard bench, staring at the same crack in the floor—maybe from a different angle. It was the place I'd told myself I wouldn't be coming back to. What made it worse was that I was missing class.

I had a choice to make: I was either going to be in the streets or go to college. I chose college. I made a vow to myself: *If I can't afford it, then I don't need it, and if I want it, I don't need it.* Stealing wasn't all that, anyhow. I was so focused on not getting caught that it often left me hungry and with a headache as time flew by while I pondered the fact that I'd wasted the last eight hours of my day being unproductive.

On the day of the court hearing, the charges were dropped and Shakira, who was my co-defendant, asked, "Want to go to South Carolina? It's sweeter up there," meaning stealing was easier, and we could make cash quickly and easily.

I was always down to ride, but this time, I had to say no. I used school as my bail out. That decision changed my life forever. Had I said yes, I would be in prison right now. That sweet deal cost Shakira twelve years of her life behind bars. I just hope they let her out sooner than later; she has a son.

"One's philosophy is not best expressed in words; it is in the choices one makes and the choices we make are ultimately our responsibility."
— **Eleanor Roosevelt**

"Less than 3% of foster youth graduate from a four-year college."
- **NFYI**

On this journey, I had to learn everything about college and what it had to offer. I also needed a more convenient job. Passing the classes wasn't the hard part; money was. I had just recently quit working at Abercrombie & Fitch. Between the expenses to travel to and from work, buying my uniform, and the pain that Chuck Taylor sneakers caused my feet, the pay wasn't worth it. So I went job hunting around campus to earn a work-study position. I had three interviews in different departments. I accepted the offer from the Institute for Civic Engagement and Democracy (ICED).

My supervisor, Dr. Erin Taylor, loves to tell a funny story about how I almost never worked at ICED. I was interested in another position that I had interviewed for. Its responsibilities included taking notes for disabled students. I told her I would be taking that position instead. But the position didn't have a guaranteed number of working hours, so if a student only had two hours of class, that was what they'd get paid for. It wasn't a good fit, as money was scarce, so I declined. I took the walk of shame back to Dr. Taylor's office to let her know I needed the position at ICED, apologizing and pleading for her to give me a chance.

We laugh about it now. It was a teachable moment. I learned to explore all opportunities and never turn down one choice until I was certain I had secured the opportunity that was right for me.

Working at ICED was the beginning of my new and improved life. The team helped me develop skills such as leadership, interviewing, public speaking, community enrichment, networking, event coordination, and more. I began to put myself out there, becoming more engaged in campus activities and taking advantage of opportunities that led to other opportunities.

I joined Trio, a student supportive services program. In addition to going to the math lab, this program offered tutoring services, which were tremendous in helping me overcome my struggles in math. In need of guidance, I joined the Single Stop Mentoring Program. As a participant, I earned the opportunity to have a mentor and build relationships with like-minded students as well as the opportunity to go on a college tour throughout the state of Florida. The trip provided great insight as I prepared for my transition to a university after earning my Associate of Arts degree.

Participation in the college tour allowed me to grow closer to the director of Single Stop, Mrs. Walton. She was a member of Rotary International Club, a network of professionals committed to taking action to create change in the community. She was interested in starting Rotaract Club, a junior chapter of Rotary, at Miami Dade College North Campus. Both clubs focus on putting community service before self. I was appointed as the club president, and she was the overseeing advisor. It was my responsibility to follow through with the application process to register Rotaract as an official club on campus. Because I was already connected with other engaged students, it wasn't difficult to establish a club board to execute activities and carry out our mission.

The Rotary Club sponsored our club T-shirts, which gave us an official look during events. Rotaract was heavily engaged in our local community. Dear to my heart, one of my favorite activities was going back to His House Children's Home. Rotaract hosted weekly fundraisers to afford catered food and have dinner with the kids living in my old group home.

Sitting at the table was emotional for me, bringing back memories of when I was in that position. I met a young girl who reminded me of myself. She appeared to be withdrawn and disconnected. She loosened up after I disclosed to her that I had once lived there. As much as I wished to tell her things would be okay, I didn't know her situation or what "okay" looked like to her. I could only reassure her that my team and I would be back to host other activities with them.

As I got more deeply involved in campus activities, my dedication to service earned me the President's Volunteer Service Award two years in a row. Thank God, this was under President Barack Obama's administration. I was issued gold medals and written letters signed by Obama himself both years. I continued to build prominent relationships, which led me to meet Suze Guillaume. She was and continues to be a good resource for all sorts of opportunities, ranging from community engagement to educational scholarships, and she even mentored me through the self-publishing process for this memoir. Suze brought to my attention scholarship opportunities provided by the Miami Foundation and the Congressional Black Caucus Foundation (CBCF), from which I benefited. But the deadline for the CBCF scholarship was less than forty-eight hours away, so I didn't have much time to apply. Despite the time constraint, I gathered all the requirements to complete the application packet, including a personal statement. Suze reviewed it and provided her feedback, and I submitted it. To my surprise, I was selected to be a recipient of the 2014 Congressional Black Caucus Scholarship, Florida District 24, which is Congresswoman Frederica Wilson's district. At the time, I didn't know much about Ms. Wilson, but I knew she was someone special to the progress of our community.

Well aware of my financial struggles in college, I found that applying to scholarships became a drug. I was told that tons of scholarship money went to waste each year because students didn't take the time to apply, so I was addicted to writing essays. I searched high and low to find scholarships and applied even if I didn't qualify. I searched specifically for scholarships for low-income, black, at-risk, and foster youth. I learned about the John H. Chafee Foster Care Independence Program,[1] but I didn't qualify due to aging out in a non-relative placement. I even typed A-list celebrity names into Google to see if they had scholarships for college students. That was how I found the Shawn Carter Student Foundation. I applied three or four years in a row. Unfortunately, I was never chosen as a recipient. I also applied for a few others, such as Foster Care 2 Success, Black Girls Rock, and the AOK Scholarship Program. I didn't get those either, but at least I'd put forth the effort. Not being selected didn't mean I wasn't the right candidate; maybe someone needed it more than me. It taught me not to be discouraged by rejection and to stay persistent and optimistic in life.

---

1 A federal program that provides financial support to foster youth pursuing post-secondary education.

"If there's one thing I've learned in life, it's the power of using your voice."
— **Michelle Obama**

After experiencing frustrations with the child welfare system, policies and procedures when submitting the tuition exemption waiver, and poor communication, I unlocked a desire for change. I finished the last class of ROTC that semester and didn't reenroll for the next. I realized my life was meant for more than just running away to the Army as an escape route. The war I wanted to fight was right here. And if I was serious about joining the cause, I needed another perspective for several reasons: to understand the operations of the system, to know why the system had caused more harm than good in my life if the whole point of it is to help children and families, and to make a difference in the lives of others who entered the system.

No child should be forced to face the same disadvantages I had faced. Children shouldn't have to endure a load of traumatic experiences, especially at no fault of their own. As a community, we should stop normalizing the mentality that we must go through the bad to get to the good. What sense does that make? The bad can lead to a life of drug dependency, suicide, or becoming the victim of another angry, violent person. If I could see the system from the inside, I'd have a better understanding, so I needed to earn the credentials to warrant a seat at the table. I scheduled a meeting with my advisor to change my major from criminal justice to social work.

I was ready to talk to professionals about things I had experienced so things other children and families wouldn't have to experience them. Professor Jamie, a social work professor at MDC, did an awesome job confirming that I had made the right choice.

Class consisted of activities that dismantled the guards I had in place preventing me from talking about my story. In teaching us about the world of social work, Professor Jamie strategically led discussions on world social issues and possible ways to solve them. He hit the touchy topic of drug abuse, and I couldn't help but think about what drugs had done to my family, using the topic to lead my engagement in class.

We even attended a field trip to Spectrum. As we toured the facility, I had flashbacks of visiting Gina. In every room of the facility, I remembered conversations or moments we'd shared. I tried to keep myself from breaking down as the program director boasted about their rehabilitation program. Angry that the program didn't work for Gina, I was able to provide insight to him about how children were affected in this situation. I remained an open book, eventually reaching a point where I accepted what had happened and gained understanding that drug addiction is a disease, that my parents were sick, and that maybe abandoning me was their best option.

If decision makers weren't going to come to me, then I would go to them. Furthering my efforts, I conducted an online search to locate an active advocacy group to immediately join while working toward earning my degree. I found Florida Youth Shine (FYS) and contacted the program coordinator, Geori Berman. She thoroughly explained the organizations mission, goals, and upcoming chapter meetings. It sounded exactly like what I was looking for.

The next Miami Chapter meeting was scheduled to meet on my birthday, October 7. I spent my twenty-first birthday at an advocacy meeting. It was the first time in a long time that I had spent my birthday doing something I wanted to do, so I considered it time well spent. Children from different agencies in Miami attended the meeting. My fellow Youth Shiners did a great job at engaging the children and explaining the work FYS had done and current legislative issues they were focusing on to present at the State Capitol. The group was exactly what I had been searching for. I was ready to sign up.

I started attending monthly and quarterly meetings to discuss issues and select specific issues the organization would tackle for the year. After identifying an issue, we'd find the legislation and dismantle it, discussing how it affected us as kids in the system and suggesting how the statute could be improved upon. We spent tons of hours bonding, planning, and prepping. Some nights were longer than others, ending with white paper plastered all over the hotel walls with colorful writings filled with ideas. Everyone had input. During prep hours, we used tools that taught us how to strategically share our stories. I found talking points helped us maximize limited time while talking to senators. We had to grab their attention, keep it, get to the point, and, with any luck, gain their support.

I had a strange run in with a senator. After a session, he suggested that I change my major to something that guarantees more money. While he offered his advice, he forgot to provide guidance on choosing an alternative major. I thought to myself, am I that good? Could I be a fierce politician in the near future? Maybe. But I did say to him, "If I don't do this job, then who will?"

Hours of preparation were essential to the time FYS spent at the State Capitol for Children's Week in Tallahassee, Florida. Over the years, Youth Shiners' stories, including my own, have resulted in the passing of several legislative changes.

Florida Statues:

39. 5085 - Relative Caregiver Fund:
> To continue the safety of children, financial resources that were only available to relatives of children have been revamped to include non-relatives of children, who are willing to assume custody and care of a dependent child as a result of a court's determination of child abuse, neglect, or abandonment.

Before this new legislation passed, non-relatives weren't eligible to receive financial assistance from the State while caring for a child. Just as finances are one of the leading causes of divorce, they were the leading issue for the disruption of non-relative placements. And the lack of support for relative and non-relative care continues to be a threatening factor for stable placements.

39.6251 – Continuing care for young adults:

The primary goal for a child in care is permanency. A child who is living in licensed care on his or her eighteenth birthday and has not achieved permanency can remain in licensed care under the jurisdiction of the court and in the care of the Department.

Before this new legislation passed, children aging out of the system were left on their own at age eighteen. It didn't matter if their permanency plan was effective or if they had the tools to be self-sufficient adults. There was no safety net for young adults to rely upon. I was in an unstable placement at the time of my emancipation. It was only a matter of time before I was kicked out. Had this law been in effect at the time of my emancipation hearing, the judge could have ordered me into licensed care, and I could have been placed in extended foster care until twenty-one years of age.

409.1454 The Keys to Independence Program: Motor vehicle insurance and driver licenses for children in care:
The cost to participate in drivers training, obtain a physical license, and get car insurance causes additional barriers for foster youth to engage in normal activities and gain independence, and it limits opportunities for obtaining employment and completing educational goals. This program intends to be a solution by reimbursing expenses.

I didn't experience issues with obtaining a permit to drive or the cost of car insurance. Driver's ed was offered in night school, and I took advantage of it to earn my permit. In my case, utilizing public transportation was more cost efficient. I didn't have money to purchase or maintain a car. Still, I was in support of this bill and able to advocate on its behalf because I understood the convenience of having reliable transportation as it relates to independence, especially in Florida, where the public transportation system isn't so efficient.

39. 5085 - Educational, Scholarships, Fees, and Financial Assistance:
While pursuing a post-secondary education, young adults were

experiencing all sorts of difficulties. Universities were operating differently across the state and putting limitations on the use of the waiver that contradicted the law. For instance, once a student reached 120 credits, including remedial and failed classes, they were no longer eligible to utilize the waiver, although Florida statute states it can be used until age twenty-eight. If a student decided to continue pursuing their degree, they would presume the cost of tuition. As a college student with an interest in pursuing higher education, it was in my best interest to support this bill and advocate for clarity in the language before it became my reality and yet another barrier.

Education is an avenue youth can take to achieve self-sufficiency and avoid lifetime dependency on government assistance. It offers unique opportunities from all walks of life. Why are there limits? Only twenty-eight states offer some form of tuition exemption for foster youth. The terms and conditions vary per state. Tuition exemption should be offered in all states, and the resource should have universal standards. The age limit should be removed due to common barriers foster youth face, even in my case. I graduated high school at nineteen years old due to legal guardianship issues and got a late start at college life. Had I lived in New Jersey, Illinois, or Connecticut, I would have had three years to earn a four-year degree because the age limit to utilize tuition exemption there is twenty-three.

TESTIMONY
Agnes Saint Preux, Former Foster Kid[1]

The term "foster child" comes with labels such as under-privileged, uneducated, abandoned, and left out. As a former foster kid, I felt the impact of a few of these labels. I entered the foster care system at the age of sixteen. A year after the death of my mother, I did not have a caregiver that was willing to care for me. While in care for two years, I had between five to six case managers and lived in both a traditional foster home and a group home as a last resort. The group home was the only available placement for my son and me. I aged out at eighteen years of age. I enrolled into the Independent Living Program and utilized the tuition waiver; however, I still felt lost and unprepared to maneuver through adulthood. No one involved in my case provided much guidance or were reliant after the fact. It was just, "Here's this program. You're eligible."

Being a child dependent on the welfare system while being a teen mom wasn't easy. I struggled. But through perseverance and determination, I learned to climb every mountain with the help of Educate Tomorrow, a program that helps create independence for disadvantaged and foster youth through education, mentoring, and life skills training. This program invested in me, showing me how to be self-sufficient in the things I wanted to do. I wanted to be a college student, so they taught me how to apply for financial aid and scholarships and gave me access to tutoring and experience to help decide on a major.

At first, submitting my tuition waiver was a headache. Every semester, I waited in the long financial aid lines just to prove, once again, I was in foster care. But that was alleviated once my school implemented a designated liaison for foster youth. Since then, my college journey has been a breeze. I have earned a bachelor's in public administration. This upcoming fall, I will be graduating with a master's in health administration.

The tuition waiver was a big help. Because of it, I didn't become just

---

1 This is the testimony of an adult that was formerly a child in the foster care system.

another statistic. I wonder what would have happened if I didn't go into foster care or have access to programs in my community where I would be. What I thought were the worst years of my life were a blessing in disguise. With trauma comes resentment, and I had to learn how to heal from being hurt and living with unanswered questions for me to move on. I am okay now. Every tear and every season of being uncomfortable contributed to the strong, educated, independent woman I am today.

I attended a few independent living classes before they were abruptly canceled. If I had a magic wand to make a change, I would bring life skill programs back to teach youth in care about the basics of adulthood, financial education, budgeting, and paying bills, and I'd add a mentoring component for youth ages twelve and up.

...

I have a voice in this world. My advocacy efforts went beyond just speaking to state legislators and gaining their support on legislative changes. I wanted to attack the grassroots of the system. This meant educating the local community on how they could be an asset to a child who was under the custody of the Department. How good is the law if the people implementing the policies are unaware of the impact of their roles?

One Saturday a month, I attended a panel discussion hosted by the Guardian Ad Litem Program.[1] Before a group of trainees, I explained my experience as a dependent of the State, and they got to pick my brain about how to be an effective GAL. They were curious to know how to go about connecting with a child. It's not rocket science. How do you greet and engage someone you've never met? Well, here's the secret sauce: Introduce yourself, explain your role, and keep your word. The last thing a child needs is for another person to lie to them. As a matter of fact, they don't need that at all, so people shouldn't volunteer if they don't have time for the gig.

I was invited to speak before law students at the University of Miami. It was an open discussion to give students insight about cases and clients they may represent during their future careers. Students took full advantage of this opportunity. They were interactive while hearing my story and applying laws as they saw fit for the scenarios, expressing how they would represent or advocate for the child.

I partnered with other organizations and joined advisory boards. Because I was a college student, Florida Reach was up my ally due to the financial aid screw up at MDC. The board discussed the benefits of having foster care liaisons present in universities to aid youth in navigating through higher education. With liaisons in place, youth would no longer have to endure the stressors of communicating with people who lacked knowledge about

---

1 Earlier, I mentioned the GAL program; at that of my life I didn't know this program existed. This opportunity had enlightened me about the role of a GAL in the dependency process. Of course, the thought crossed my mind. Why wasn't I assigned a GAL to speak in my best interest?

the tuition exemption waiver or the unnecessary red tape of resubmitting verification every semester to show they were, indeed, wards of the State. The initiative was successfully implemented throughout colleges in the state of Florida, and I utilized this resource throughout my college career. I remember going back and forth with an employee at Florida International University about the fees associated with earning a certificate in human resources policy and management to complement my master's degree. I simply advised the liaison at Fostering Panther Pride, and the issue was resolved.

"I made it! Don't sit down and wait for the opportunities to come.
Get up and make them."
— **Madame CJ Walker**

Children's Week was more than walking the halls and advocating to state legislators. Agencies from all regions of the state were in town to celebrate successes over a fancy five-course dinner at Florida State University, served by an upscale catering company. FYS Mentors provided etiquette training to the youth before the dinner to avoid embarrassing moments.

It was a time to network by mingling and getting to know some key players. For anyone serious about getting their foot into the field of social work, the next opportunity was in that room. I was in the midst of preparing to graduate from Miami Dade with an Associate in Arts degree, which meant the end of my work-study position was approaching. And I'd be unemployed. An introduction to the CEO of Florida Foster Care Review (FFCR) couldn't have come at a more perfect time. While chatting, the CEO let me know about a possible employment opportunity.

Upon returning to Miami, I followed up with an e-mail to schedule an interview and was eventually hired as a file specialist. I spent fifteen hours a week transitioning physical case files into an electronic system, familiarizing myself with child welfare language and informing youth about their right to a judicial review social study report (JRSSR).[2] The JRSSR is a legally binding document that details the status of a case. It's completed by the dependency case manager and submitted to the courts to ensure professionals and parents are in compliance with their case plan,[3] the child's needs are met, and the case

---

2 **s. 39.701 Judicial Review** — (a) The court shall have continuing jurisdiction in accordance with this section and shall review the status of the child's well-being and case at least every 6 months as required by this subsection or more frequently if the court deems it necessary or desirable.

3 **s. 39.6011 Case Plan Development** — The department shall prepare a draft document for each child receiving services. A detailed description and logistics of each service should be included. Parents must participate in the process. This document must be approved by the courts.

is progressing toward the permanency goal. Based on this report, professionals can inquire about any concerns and make necessary recommendations.

My time at FFCR ended earlier than intended. The initial goal was to work there until it was time for me to transition to Florida State University for the upcoming school year, but my dedication to advocacy earned me a trip across state lines. That summer, I was looking to spread my wings. I applied to complete an internship with Congressional Caucus Adoption Institute. I wrote a compelling essay, including my experience and highlighting the need for children in care to have legal representation of their own. I wasn't selected. But for every no, another opportunity is opened. Keeping my options open, I applied to several other internships and was chosen to intern with Foster Club in Seaside, Oregon as an All-Star.

I quickly advanced to become a traveling advocate. I traveled to other cities within Oregon to inspire and engage with youth. I also traveled to Washington D.C to attend the White House Champion of Change event. It was my first time stepping foot inside the White House. I was hoping to see the Obamas, but I wasn't that lucky. On the Hill, I met with senators to discuss my experience living in group homes.

Advocating was therapeutic, a safe space. I could be my true self and talk about things I'd held hostage for so long. It was a relief. It felt like a heavy load was being lifted off my soul. I didn't have to worry about being ashamed, called a liar, or being recommended for a psychiatric evaluation. My ideas and opinions were not shut out and were considered helpful to others. Because of that, no one could get me to shut up.

I had mastered speaking but looked to community leaders and mentors to gain experience to advance my skills in human services, advocacy, and politics as a dynamic and diverse professional. When opportunities to learn presented themselves, I took full advantage. After applying to participate in Foster Youth Shadow Day with the National Foster Youth Institute alongside a member of the Congressional Black Caucus and not being selected in 2014, I tried again in 2015 and was paired with Congresswoman Frederica Wilson. Shadowing Ms. Wilson, I observed her fierce delivery as she supported the financial upkeep provided to federal and postal employees who were injured or killed on the job and their families. The committee meeting debated about continuing or discontinuing the subsidy of these workers without alternative options for income. The heartfelt testimonies of the medically retired and disabled individuals and spouses of deceased workers swayed the committee, which resulted in favorable outcomes.

I watched a limbless man plead before the committee to maintain his source of income. Ms. Wilson and I shared frustration. Why was slashing this program's funding even being considered? These people's lives had been affected forever during the delivery of services that benefited the operations of this country. In a separate room, Ms. Wilson delivered an empathic speech, apologizing for the threat posed to their livelihoods and her gratitude for the workers' dedication to service. She ensured the group that she would support this topic and fight whenever necessary. She exemplified the kind of public servant I desired to be: bold, knowledgeable, and effective.

*"Just try new things. Don't be afraid. Step out of your comfort zones
and soar, all right?"*
— **Michelle Obama**

On the fun side, Oregon was different. It was not like anything I was used to. Before packing, I had asked what I needed to bring, and I was clearly advised that it was summertime in Seaside. Summertime to me meant hot, sweaty, halter tops, and icy-flavored treats. I packed my luggage like I was spending the summer in Miami. I was completely wrong. I realized that summer in Seaside was, to me, winter. I had to have a friend of mine ship a package including sweaters, scarves, and boots. It was my first culture shock.

I was surprised to see natives enjoying the freezing water of the Pacific Ocean. I thought, *Are y'all crazy? It's cold out here! Yeah, they're crazy and going to be sick!* I found joy in doing more weather-permitted activities such as my very first bonfire. Over the flames of burning wood, I sandwiched honey graham crackers and marshmallows. I'm not a fan of chocolate.

Feeling adventurous, I took a hike. The other interns ranted about a scene from the movie *The Goonies* that was shot on a nearby mountain. So to experience it ourselves, we took a hike. Standing on the edge of the mountain and looking over the top into the ocean, I witnessed a view I had only seen on television. With my heart beating, afraid that I might fall, I looked. But what started as a friendly activity turned into an exhausting, regretful adventure. One of the interns had claimed he didn't want to go on the hike but later changed his mind. He didn't follow the trail. He entered the mountain through a back way and got lost. With limited resources and dying cellphones, some of us decided to go find him. I regret making the decision. Walking through the mountain, I felt the different climate changes. It was either misty, rainy, or hot. I destroyed a favorite pair of boots. They were covered in mud inside and out. It took us hours to find him. And when we did, we still had to find our way out of the mountain. Even more hours passed. Once we found our way out, we were in another city at a different beach, and nighttime had fallen. Just when we thought we'd reached salvation, the road out of the park was yet another journey. We had no other choice but to keep going until I saw a sign warning about the presence of jaguars, bears, or lions. (I don't remember which wild animal it was, but I do remember I was terrified.) There was no way I was walking an unprotected path with vicious animals on the loose.

There are some nice people in Oregon. After a few cars drove past us, one finally stopped and gave us a ride. They told us the road was miles long and not walking distance. We'd been saved! They dropped us off at a nearby store, and a staff member from Foster Club came to get us. It was an experience of a lifetime. All the different views throughout the mountain were unforgettable. Luckily, I can scratch hiking off my bucket list. I'm never doing that again.

"Keep going no matter what."
— **Reginald Lewis**

I graduated with honors, earning an Associate of Arts degree. Miami Dade College knew how to host a celebration. Graduation was fun, more like a party versus the traditional boring, long ceremony. Even more special, a reporter from the Miami Herald was present, specifically, to interview me. The reporter highlighted my graduation, explaining how I had overcome the hard knocks of foster care and discussing the benefits of having access to support groups and resources. The full article is on the website at www.miamiherald.com, titled "The Affordable Care Act Gives Former Foster Kids Healthcare Benefits to Age 26, Though They May Not Know It."

After aging out of foster care, I no longer had health insurance. Once the new law went into effect, I had first-hand knowledge of insurance and assistance, completing the application without hiccups in the process. At twenty-three, I was able to attend my annual check-ups and semi-annual dental cleanings with the cost covered by insurance.

But even in the happiest moments, the uninvited feeling of disappointment found its way to the party. I had invited two close friends to celebrate the moment with me. They were aware of everything I'd been through and how sensitive I could be about people not showing up. What others may have thought was minor was big to me. Already suppressing the emotions triggered by previous letdowns, I now had to deal with the disappointment of their no-show. They claimed to have come to the ceremony, but I never saw them. Their excuse for not finding me after the ceremony was poor cell phone service. They missed the photo op and had another excuse for why they couldn't make it to dinner.

My anxiety was beginning to sizzle, and I had to snap out of it. I wanted my loved ones to share the front page of the newspaper with me, but it didn't happen. It was just Mylika and me. I learned to live by a new ideology: Those who want to be present, will show, and those who don't will make excuses.

No matter what, I will enjoy my moment. After graduation, my sisters, Dr. Taylor, and I celebrated my success at Bubba Gump Shrimp Co.

Even after Brooke had kicked me out of her home, I was still open to having a relationship with her when the opportunity arose. But her constant disrespect led me to ultimately end the relationship.

The first incident was about her buying her daughter a birthday cake. She'd asked to use my food stamp card to buy the cake, and I said yes, even though I used food stamps to contribute to Ashley's household. But she had unrealistic expectations. She wanted me to travel on the bus to Publix and hand deliver the cake. I was more than willing to buy the cake, but I didn't have a car, and taking the bus was further inconvenience. I suggested that her boyfriend come to pick up the card and cake, but his license was suspended. Rudely, she mentioned my friends helping me to return favors I had done for them. My friends had nothing to do with it. Why should I have had to pay them for gas? She was being unreasonable, considering she had a car of her own.

Next, I borrowed her cooler for a college fundraising event. I had no intentions of keeping it, but before I could return it, she became disrespectful in her efforts to get it back, sending me an impolite, lengthy text message. I don't remember why she was upset, but I made it my business to give her the cooler the next day. I was fed up with her expectations and disrespect and began to distance myself.

The night before my graduation from Miami Dade College, Brooke randomly called my phone, complaining about not receiving an invitation. I wasn't really listening to her scream through the phone, but I did grasp the main point of her complaint. I told her I would have my sister deliver her a graduation ticket in the morning. Since graduates were required to be at the ceremony's location five hours before the ceremony started, I was unable to do it myself.

Although Brooke was a no-show at the ceremony, she made her presence known by tagging me in an intriguing Facebook post:

In life u have to make the right decision "at first" when it matters the most, not when you think it counts "at the last minute" .... I know I did a great job from way down in under n it shows!!! Kenisha E. Anthony today is ur day shine bright like a diamond baby girl it's a whole world out her waiting to give u lesson about life..... #ipatmyselfontheback #startedfromthebottom #nalwaysbeenhere in my drake voice,

Surprisingly, the post is still there today. During the ceremony, I didn't finish reading it before disregarding it and continuing to enjoy the fruits of my labor. *Some mother*, I thought.

After the ceremony, my sister told me she had attempted to deliver the ticket, but Brooke said, "She don't have anyone else to give this ticket to, because I'm not coming."

I was confused. Why had she called me? I didn't know, but from the looks of it, she was trying to hurt me. She could have just left me alone if she already knew she wasn't coming. A mother should never take that type of approach to resolve an issue. If she had genuinely wanted to attend the ceremony, she would have, regardless of the timing. I was over it and decided to put our relationship in the grave once and for all. I wouldn't beg for respect or force anyone to be a part of my life. I took part of the blame for allowing her to let me down once again.

Over the years, people have shared with me that she walks around the city boasting about having made me who I am, saying that if it wasn't for her, I wouldn't be in the position I am today. As good as that sounds, it can't be true. One person cannot make another in that sense. People contribute to your journey, in either a good or bad way, but they don't make you. "I make me." I don't have a clue as to why she feels she deserves that level of recognition. I wholeheartedly disagree. As much as I wish her tales of support were true, they are not.

As more years passed, she tried reaching out to me. She wrote me on Facebook, claiming to need to speak with me ASAP. Because we're not friends on the site, her message went to the request box, a section of the direct message inbox of which I had no knowledge. It just so happened that one day while stopping for food, I bumped into her daughter and a family friend, Esha. Esha asked if I had received Brooke's message. At the time, I hadn't. Esha explained why Brooke desperately needed to speak with me. Her daughter was allegedly having behavior problems, and she blamed her bad behavior on my absence, claiming her daughter felt I had turned my back on her.

I hesitated. This was foreign to me because her daughter and I had never had a sisterly bond. But it's never my intention to treat people the way others treated me, so I turned to her daughter and extended myself. "We can have a relationship but with boundaries. I do not wish to have a relationship with your mom," I said.

Esha asked, "Did you ever feel like Brooke was a mother to you?"

"No, because she wasn't."

My living under her roof didn't make her my mother. I didn't want to revisit the past. A relationship can't be mended until what was broken is addressed. And I wasn't willing to do that. I had moved on with life.

Well, her daughter wasn't happy with my response. She said, "Fuck you" and some other words to defend her mom.

With no regrets, I smiled, returned to my car, and continued my day. I thought, *When I had issues, she talked down about me and kicked me out of her house. Now that her daughter is a teenager and having issues, she wants my help.* The irony. That confirmed it. People will never treat you like they treat their own children.

I was in a better position. I received acceptance letters from Florida International University, Florida Atlantic University, the University of West Florida, and Florida State University (FSU) after receiving denial letters two years ago. I had options and chose to take my talents to the prestigious FSU. Getting accepted into FSU felt like a dream. In high school, I didn't bother applying to Florida State. After searching their website and reviewing the admissions statistics and requirements, it was clear to me that I wasn't smart enough to get accepted, even with the grace of affirmative action. I didn't have a chance. But times had changed. I had something to look forward to.

I'd been accepted into one of the top universities in the State of Florida; who would have thought? It was an accomplishment that deserved to be celebrated, so I planned to do just that in preparation for my transition to Tallahassee. Like every student, I wanted to have a trunk party, and I chose a bowling theme.

A part of me was skeptical. My interest in having any kind of event to celebrate myself had died years ago. It was always the same game. When I wanted to do something, plans never worked out or people I had invited were no-shows. I had tried having a pool party for my fifteenth birthday that resulted in a disaster. Only one of my friends showed, and instead of my family embracing the day, they laughed and made jokes about me not having friends. To save myself from future embarrassment, I had put the idea of parties to rest. I'd rather spend a day with myself versus being the laughingstock again.

But this time in my life was different. I had loved ones, mostly friends I considered family. I thought that with them in my life, the party would have a good turnout. I created a college registry with Bed, Bath & Beyond, made reservations at Sparez Bowling, and sent out invitations. I consulted with everyone about the event, letting them know that the cost of food and bowling lanes was paid. Adults can be competitive during bowling, so I made the event kid-friendly and accommodated them by purchasing a few lanes for their children to attend, relieving them from having to find babysitters and using that as an excuse for why they couldn't come to the party. Guests were only required to show up and bring a gift that would be beneficial toward my education or off-campus apartment. I mean, that was the whole purpose of having a trunk party.

Even with RSVP's, less than ten guests showed, some late and without gifts. I was appreciative that they'd come, but it was a waste of my hard-earned money that could've gone toward my college needs versus trying to share a moment with people.

I had this weird thing about being hopeful, wanting to feel loved, and trying to live a normal life, one with a family, even if it meant building relationships to create one. But it tended to feel like I was always being forced to settle, just take what I could get. Nothing could make people put forth effort when it was about me, not even graduation or going off to college.

The smallest thing was a trigger. I felt unimportant and disregarded once again. The feelings of abandonment overwhelmed me, and I beat myself up for having poor judgement, creating another opportunity to be disappointed. And as the day went on, it got worse. Tiffany was drunk and started saying crazy things. I don't remember exactly what she was talking about, but it made me mad, so mad that I instructed somebody to get her before I punched her for embarrassing me. She tended to act wild and senseless to be the center of attention, making things all about her. Instead of slapping her, I left my own party. The next day, my advisor called and told me she'd driven Tiff home. I was more pissed off. During the ride, she was ranting about her boyfriend, love, pain, her mom, and other stuff. I was embarrassed and speechless and could only apologize for her behavior, thinking she had only done it to receive the attention she was seeking.

At times when I felt weary, something came along to get my spirits back up. Because I was connected to FYS and dedicated to excelling in academics, Geori recommended me for the Emy's Promise Scholarship Program. The organization reached out in search of a young lady headed to college. I learned another important skill: how to evaluate finances. Going away to college meant a new set of financial responsibilities. I had to provide my financial aid award package and a detailed budget, which I hadn't put much thought into, but the spreadsheet they provided helped put things in perspective. It included expenses not limited to housing, books, school supplies, utilities, transportation, telephone, Internet, toiletries, and food. Expenses my financial aid wouldn't cover for the entire semester. I was still a low-income college student. And I didn't have a job awaiting my arrival. Emy's Promise provided an educational scholarship to contribute to the relief of any financial burdens I may have experienced and afforded me the opportunity to focus on my coursework to achieve my educational goals. The scholarship was renewable throughout my college career.

After spending the summer in Oregon, I returned to Miami with only two days to transition and kick-off the fall semester. The plan was for Ashely to get a rental car to drop me off at school with my belongings. However, it didn't happen. I don't know why she hadn't reserved it early on, but because she had waited, the rates increased. And I was not willing to pay the rental fee for being underage. My expectation for the off-to-college road trip experience was ruined. In a desperate measure, I packed two suitcases to capacity and purchased a Greyhound bus ticket.

I was still looking forward to experiencing a normal life. As I suffered from disappointment on the bus ride, my emotions were raging. I felt the tears coming. My parents were absent, I didn't have all my belongings, and I was by my lonesome, relocating to an unfamiliar place. I pondered why Ashley hadn't made proper arrangements to drop me off at college.

The bus was expected to arrive right before the crack of dawn. I hadn't made travel plans to get to my apartment. For all I knew, I was going to have to catch a cab. And due to all the creepy, weird people in the world, I feared riding alone with strangers. I'm a petite person and some may view me as an easy target. But with the help of Lily, a former foster youth I had met in Oregon, catching a cab was the least of my worries. I contacted her, explained the situation, and asked her for assistance. Lily was more than willing to help, and she picked me up from the train station.

Upon arrival, it was still early. Check-in time at The Boulevard off-campus student housing wasn't until 10 a.m. I waited around, but Lily had to work and wouldn't return home until late in the evening. I remembered that when I had announced on Facebook that I was going to FSU, one of Ashley's paternal cousins commented on the post, stating that she lived in Tallahassee, so I contacted her via Facebook and, with her help, transitioned into my furnished apartment. I was still a little upset, but it worked out in the end. I just hated that everything had to be a struggle.

I chose to stay off campus because I wanted my own space for a change. I grew tired of sharing and didn't want any distractions caused by unnecessary human interaction. The more personally styled on-campus dorms were designated for graduate students, and the other dorms shared one bathroom for the floor. I didn't want that.

My credit wasn't yet established, so The Boulevard rejected my application for an apartment unless I returned with a co-signer. I asked Ashley, who was working on fixing her credit, thinking I may still get rejected, but she was hesitant to sign because if I missed a payment, she would be held responsible. I tried showing the exemption waiver, explaining that I was a ward of the State, independent, and didn't have that kind of support. The property manager didn't have a clue about foster kids and the circumstances they faced while pursuing secondary education. Although I still needed a co-signer, I was able to enlighten them about the subject and helped them understand that the chances of a foster youth in college having a co-signer was slim. I was nervous because if Ashley said no or didn't pass the background check, I'd have no one else to turn to. It wasn't like the option to go before a judge to request a court order for the matter was available. But because of all the back and forth, Ashley agreed to co-sign. She passed the screening, and I was thankful.

Everything worked itself out. I adjusted and looked forward to being an official Seminole. Certain things were simple, such as the shuttle to school that picked students up in front of the apartment complex. But other things were difficult like not having a car, which made it a challenge to go shopping for groceries or household necessities. I couldn't always depend on my roommate, who was a pharmacy student at FAMU. She was always studying. And Ashley's cousin wasn't that much help after moving in. I text messaged her and never received a response. I didn't want to be a burden for anyone, so I didn't explore that avenue again. I don't even know if Uber was a thing at the time, but my fear of riding in cars with strangers wouldn't have allowed me to give that idea much thought. I'd catch the bus to the nearest Publix to get things like milk, bread, and seasonings. Then I'd go to the school pantry to get food such as canned goods, pastas, and microwave dishes.

I made do with the circumstances. And the more situations occurred, the more innovative I tried to be. I thought I had a plan to get to work figured out. Considering my budget, I would ride the bus to a specific location, which was the easy part, and ride my bike the rest of the way. What I didn't know was that Tallahassee was known for hills and bugs I'd never seen before. While riding up the side of the main road, ants started biting me, so I took the nearest back road. Following my GPS, I had no clue where I was traveling. All the roads led to dead ends. I was frustrated, late, and had wasted time with this brilliant idea. Before I knew it, I was in the middle of the road with the bike lying beside me, experiencing a mental breakdown. I had been overwhelmed with emotions since the rental car incident, thinking of what my life would've been like if I'd had supportive parents.

Even with the aid of resources and support from others, the scar of abandonment was still present. I wanted my parents. It was those personal situations that aroused the triggers, situations that no program could heal. In the middle of that road alone, I was reminded that I needed my parents. I could only imagine how different that moment would have been if I'd had their support. I cried, wondering why everything had to be a struggle. Why wasn't I important to them? How could they live without being a part of my life? I was a child to be proud of.

But I could only allow myself ten minutes to drown in pity before picking myself up to keep going. I contacted my supervisor for guidance. He was able to pinpoint my location and provide directions to work. Lesson learned: my beach cruiser was only for campus use.

With connections to the foster care world, I was selected to participate in a pilot program to help foster children gain employment and learn skills. The state legislature and governor approved a $75,000 budget and partnered with the Florida Department of Agriculture to conduct the program. The program was necessary for young adults, and beneficial. One of the participants was lucky; she was a Tallahassee native and gained full-time employment with the state of Florida. For me, the program was just a steppingstone. I was placed in the wildlife section of the department. Most projects focused on trees, forests, and plants, subjects I only appreciated in my spare time for the scenery and pictures.

The fall semester had its ups and downs, emotionally. I struggled with completing assignments detailing my family tree and refused to live a week below the poverty line. My professor wanted us to understand the struggles of those who live day by day on a fixed income. She had specific instructions. I only remember things such as students could only eat rice, beans, and/ or bread; sleep anywhere other than their bed; utilize public transportation; and not spend over a specified dollar amount. I disclosed to her that a week of these activities was a trigger for me. She allowed me to opt out of the assignment and write a two-page paper about my personal experiences. I managed to make the dean's list, earning a B, B+, and two A's. And during the Christmas break, I planned to purchase a car with the money I'd saved over the last five months. Over the years, I'd spent time building up credit with the use of a secured card. Credit was important, and I knew my chances of having a co-signer were slim, so I decided to freeze $500 from one of my financial aid refund checks on a secured card and use it as a credit card. I met with a financial advisor at the bank to learn the rules of credit and followed them, ensuring that I never surpassed 30 percent and made on-time payments. I used the card only for mandatory purchases such as hygiene products. After practicing those habits for so long, I thought I'd established a trusting relationship with my bank, and they would be more than willing to approve me for a car loan. That was partly true. I had good, but limited credit. I had never heard of that term; it meant no one had ever trusted me with a large amount of money, so they wouldn't either unless I had a co-signer and a deposit. I had the deposit but not the co-signer, and they weren't willing to negotiate. Neither was Ashley. She had no interest in co-signing a car loan. I was frustrated, thinking about how rough it was to live in Tallahassee without a car.

Ashley suggested I try Auto Nation and get a vehicle under $10,000. I had $3,000 to put down. It was just my luck; I found a 2008 Honda Civic coupe for $11,000. The salesman sensed I was ready to purchase. He wasn't going to miss out on his commission and was willing to deduct $1,000 to accommodate my budget, a budget I was not willing to adjust. Ashely and

I prayed and stayed positive while the salesman went to consult with his manager. He returned with a decision: I was approved with a $2,700 deposit. I don't recall the amount of the car payment, but I told myself I'd pay $250 a month. With the remaining $300, I paid for car insurance to drive off the car lot that day. Upon receiving financial aid in the spring, I paid the insurance in full for the six-month term resulting in a discount, and I received some of the money back.

"It's not the load that breaks you down; it's the way you carry it."
— **Lena Horne**

Returning to college was smooth, with the remainder of my belongings and a car. Being more fluid, I had more time, eliminating the time spent catching public transportation. Most of my days were spent being a student, working, and participating in FYS festivities. In addition to the position at the Department of Agriculture, I committed to conducting ten hours per week of research for a PhD social work professor, focusing on child traumatization. An FSU professor who attended FYS meetings had referred me to the paid position.

Tallahassee is known for parties, but I didn't have much time for extracurricular activities, or maybe I just wasn't interested. I'd outgrown the party life as a teenager, when I had enjoyed the Miami nightlife in both adult and teen clubs. I grew to be an overachiever, so even when classmates extended an invitation to hang out, I passed with the exception of two outings. After listening to them whine about me being boring, I hung out with them at a chicken and waffle event hosted by Sistahs Inc. Then we chilled later that same evening at a local bar. That was the extent of my party life as a college student.

I found joy in new experiences, so although I didn't party much, I did attend campus events hosted by the Center for Global Engagement and Center for Leadership and Social Change. The events were of interest as I learned about cultures, people, and environments different from my own. International Tea Hour was designed for students to become culturally competent and learn how the Japanese culture prepared and served tea. I was amazed that it really did take a full hour to prepare, serve, and enjoy a cup of tea. The usual time for me was no longer than fifteen minutes, and I couldn't forget to add a cube of sugar. But the Japanese do it differently. They place a piece of candy on the back of their tongues as a sweetener then drink the tea. It was different, not so much to my liking but fun to at least try it. I would do it again.

Scrolling on Instagram, I ran across a woman's page that aligned with my interests. The page was appealing. I knew she wasn't faking a lifestyle on Instagram because she was my maternal niece and my paternal cousin's girlfriend. I struggled even saying that out loud, but she was real. She was classy and inspiring, pursuing her dream as an interior designer, traveling around the world, tasting different kinds of food, and capturing fine pictures of her adventures. She was a reader as well. After seeing her post the book Eat Pray Love by Elizabeth Gilbert, I decided to check it out. As a participant in the program with the International Student Foundation, I had the option to read a book alongside my mentor, so I took that opportunity to get my hands on the book.

In the book, Elizabeth uses her trauma as a devastated newly divorced woman to share her journey and move on from the life she once knew. With the last bit of money in her bank account, she travels to three counties that began with the letter I—Indonesia, Italy, and India—in search of peace and happiness. An important key on her healing journey is to never let money be an issue, and everything will work itself out. To reach a place of serenity, Elizabeth practices yoga and works hard to reap the benefits of meditation. She struggles along the way but keeps trying until she eventually masters it. By the end of the book, I was fascinated by Elizabeth's lifestyle and wanted to experience a spiritual journey of my own, from pain to peace. I wanted to move on from my life of being emotionally and mentally disturbed, suffering from abandonment and abuse. I wanted to reinvent myself and reintroduce myself to this world. At the end of the journey, I would be relieved from the label of broken and bitter child.

Because it was included in the cost of tuition, I signed up for free on-campus yoga, cycling, and personal training, adding fitness goals to my journey. As an early bird, I always did the 6 a.m. yoga session before the start of my first class. Morning yoga helped me focus my energy and thoughts to prepare for a peaceful and productive day. I practiced mediation at home with the aid of Oprah and Deepak Chopra's Meditation Experience. I also signed up to receive Oprah's newsletters, reaping the benefits of the thoughts of the day, healthy eating habits, and self-care tips. Cycling sessions were mostly held in the evening. I fell the first time I mounted the bike as I tried to gain control of the pedals. I was a beginner and out of shape, but that was a good thing, the more pain the better. It helped to refocus the emotional pain I felt in my chest to the pain in my thighs. To the beat of "Run the World" by Beyoncé, I envisioned every foot stroke as a piece of depression and anxiety being released through breathing techniques. The lyrics gave me my momentum.

I was empowered. Pairing music with cycling made the perfect combination. After every session, I felt closer to achieving a major accomplishment. I felt better. On a random day, I felt so good that I checked out a baseball game just to experience it once in my lifetime. It was on campus and free. All I needed to show was my ID, confirming I was a student at FSU.

Continuing my spiritual journey, I jammed to albums by J. Cole, John Legend, and Aloe Blacc. On 2014 *Forest Hills Drive*, J. Cole questioned if I wanted to be happy and free from pain and scars. John Legend's *Love in the Future* questioned my ability to love myself again and asked what was going on in my beautiful mind. And Aloe Blacc's Lift Your Spirit tested my faith, explaining to me that life was a test to which I should give my best and God made my mold different from the rest. These albums were on rotation and served as a reminder to the place I was striving to reach.

With Elizabeth's philosophy of not letting money get in my way, I listened and took a leap of faith. I thought it was the craziest idea. Elizabeth was probably in a different tax bracket than I was, but I found the perfect chance to study abroad with the College of Social Work in Europe and visit countries such as the Czech Republic, Germany, and Poland to study communism and the Holocaust. It was a win-win opportunity. I'd get to travel to new places, experience different environments and cultures, earn college credits, and graduate a semester early.

To start the process, I applied for a passport, which arrived in less than a month; paid the application fee; created a GoFundMe campaign; and applied for international scholarships. I also continued working and saving to study abroad. After paying the $100 application fee and raising enough money to cover the cost of the $250 commitment fee, I was empowered to pull it off.

The next step was to tackle the program fee: $5,853. I applied for the Gilman and CSW International Scholarships. I was selected to receive the CSW International Scholarship; however, I was placed on the alternative list for the Gilman International Scholarship. The amount of the Gilman scholarship was unknown, but the program was known for giving students large awards, so I kept my fingers crossed. In the meantime, I had to figure out how I was going to pay the remaining balance of $4,300 and daily expenses.

Florida Children's First had chosen to honor me as Youth Advocate of the Year and awarded me a proclamation for my dedication to advocating for change in the child welfare system. In acceptance of my award, I delivered a thank you speech, mentioning long-term and short-term aspirations. My dear friend Howard took the floor and delivered an elevator pitch, encouraging the group to invest in the dreams of ambitious young people like me because it gave hope for a better tomorrow, and he concluded his speech with a fundraiser. By the end of the night, I was closer to reaching the program fee cost.

His speech and the resulting support were medicine to relieve the frustration stemming from hearing another set of last-minute excuses and sitting at a reserved dinner table by my lonesome. None of my invited guests showed. I was embarrassed when asked about their whereabouts, brushing off the conversation with a resolve to just enjoy the evening.

After a few days, maybe a week, had passed, my phone rang. It was a call from Geori. An anonymous donor had come forward to pay most of the fee, donating a little over $3,000. Even closer to achieving the goal, Emy's Promise awarded me a study abroad scholarship, eliminating the remaining balance. With the program fee out of the way, my focus turned to the cost of food, travel, excursions, and any additional money I'd need to reap the benefits this trip had to offer.

I purchased a round-trip flight for $1,200 while awaiting a response from Gilman. Finally, the Gilman Scholarship Program notified me that I hadn't been selected for an award. It was a huge disappointment. *I thought, Well, I'll just be on a budget, but I'll still get to experience places I've never been before.* It was a positive perspective.

My mentors from Emy's Promise recommended I apply for a Capitol One credit card because it didn't have international fees. I did and was approved for $1,000. I thought it would hold me over along with my savings for the trip.

On a phone call with Dr. Taylor, I was whining about not being selected for the Gilman scholarship and my current financial position for the trip. She reassured me with words of encouragement. "You've made it this far. It's meant to be, and everything will work itself out."

Just as she said those words to me, an e-mail notification buzzed my phone. It was another message from Gilman, informing me that I was, in fact, selected as a recipient of the Benjamin A. Gilman International Scholarship. Dr. Taylor was still on the phone, and I advised her to disregard everything I had just said. I received a $3,500 scholarship from Gilman to study abroad. After the Obama ordeal, this was the second time in life I claimed to have good luck. But this was more than just luck; it was a moment when hard work met opportunity and paid off. What was for me was for me! It was final—I was going to Europe!

*"Change will not come if we wait for some other person or some time.
We are the ones we've been waiting for. We are the change that we seek."*
— **Barack Obama**

Before boarding the plane to Europe, I had two things to do: pass summer classes and secure an internship to satisfy graduation requirements. To my advantage, the School of Social Work assigned field officers to help students secure an internship. While reviewing the variety of organizations with which FSU had connections, one caught my eye: Building Resilience Center (BRC). As a kid, I had attended their Christmas holiday event and received a Wal-Mart gift card. It was only ten dollars, but it was something. This was my chance to gain experience and peek inside the system, providing me the gateway to understanding what happened to my family. I submitted a cover letter and résumé and awaited a response from the field supervisor, Monique, who was also a program operations administrator (POA), to set up an interview.

My time in Tallahassee had come to an end, and I had no intention of remaining or returning to the city. I moved out early to avoid paying the last month of rent and utilities before my lease expired. The Boulevard gave tenants that option, so I took advantage of the offer, packed my belongings into my two-door coupe, and headed back to Miami. I finished the first half of summer courses with two A's and I would complete the other two classes abroad, earning two additional A's with a cumulative GPA of 3.808.

In the meantime, I was in preparation mode, shopping and packing my luggage for the trip and preparing to interview for the internship. Everything went as planned, and some things happened unexpectedly. I explored many attractions while in Europe. The trip included two long weekends that allowed me to travel to other countries. I battled the choice between Greece, France, and Amsterdam or just staying in Prague. One weekend, I chose to go to France and saw the Love Lock Bridge and the Eiffel Tower, and I rode the train in the conductor's station because I got lost on my way to the Louvre. The second weekend, I stayed in Prague. I didn't have any prior knowledge about the country before the trip, so I decided to go sightseeing on my own time. I was just following the tourist attraction guide and happened to stumble across the John Lennon Wall, enjoying it for a cute photo op. I had heard about the Beatles and knew he was a musician, but what I didn't know about John was that he was in foster care. I never expected to visit John Lennon's memorial and meet his sister, Julia, upon returning to the States. I was invited to an event to celebrate the rock band and got the honor to talk with her after the show. She shared her and John's story about being removed from their parents and living in relative care with an abusive aunt and being removed from her as well. She also told me about pursuing her passion to help disadvantaged children like us. Collectively, we chimed in to share our struggles and emotions, such as being disappointed, scared to trust again, and having to protect and fend for ourselves.

God's timing, with one event right after the other, blew my mind. He was sending a message, aligning me to my purpose, and I received it. The power in hearing the experiences of other foster youth confirmed that my feelings were normal, and they were something I could overcome. Listening to how Julia had managed to turn her pain into passion and share that same desire, I knew it was possible for me, too, and I was on the right road.

During the last semester of undergraduate studies as an intern with one class remaining, I had two goals: graduate and learn as much as I could to earn a full-time position with a foster care agency.

For my agency internship, Monique assigned me to unit 824, then the unit supervisor assigned me directly under a certified case manager to learn everyday functions of case management. Chanel was nice but firm and managed her caseload well. Her clients loved her, even when she had to follow protocol due to their non-compliant behavior. Before resigning, she taught me everything she knew: how to be an effective case manager, time management, service providers, utilizing support workers, and maintaining sanity while tending to the needs of others. She was honest about the demands of the job and its high-level stress factors. Because I didn't have children or a husband at home, she was positive that I would do fine.

While Chanel appeared to have a handle on her caseload, other case managers expressed heavy frustration. If it wasn't one thing, it was a mixture of things that required immediate attention—a troubled child, completion of a court document, home visits, transportation, supervised visitation, client services, and a demanding administrator. I've witnessed case managers resign during training, immediately after training, or after a few weeks on the job. Those who complained but chose to tough it out were already planning their exit. I thought the real issue was that they lacked passion and didn't have intentions to do the job from the start. People doing a job just for a paycheck. For what other reason would they quit so soon? From the eyes of an intern, I thought the solution was as simple as being organized and practicing effective time management skills, placing the blame on the case managers for procrastination. I thought, *When I become a case manager, I don't want to be like them, and I'll do a better job.*

The internship was coming to an end, and graduation was approaching. I was prepared to transition into my career. The case management position was in high demand year round. With minimal experience, I submitted applications to each agency in the South Florida area. There was gossip about agencies that paid more money and implemented case caps, the maximum number of cases that can be assigned to a case manager at one time. Others countered the gossip, advising that it was the same no matter which agency we chose. I considered opinions from professionals in the field. One of the agencies lost their contract due to mismanagement of cases and falsifying records, among other problems. The agencies differed because the one where I was interning wasn't undergoing those kinds of issues, so I kept an open mind and focused on getting my foot in the door.

Despite repeatedly being told I would hate the job and seeing some of its flaws, I wasn't deterred from pursuing my goal. If I wanted to understand the system and see change, I had to join in. I couldn't keep on complaining and expect others to be the change I wanted to see. I informed Monique of my interest in becoming a case manager, completed an interview, and locked in a full-time position before graduating with a bachelor's degree in social work.

The moment I'd been working for was reality, despite what others had projected over my life: drug abuse, prostitution, dropping out of high school, becoming a career thief, and whatever else they thought. Statistics project that less than 3 percent of youth that age out of foster care will graduate high school. For those who do and choose to pursue secondary education, less than 1 percent will graduate. It continues to be a highly utilized statistic that often gave me anxiety as I questioned which side of the statistics would define me. But there I was, beating the odds as an independent black woman and a college graduate, proving them wrong, proving myself and the statistics wrong. This moment was about more; it was a time to be proud of myself and celebrate my success. As I sat among other graduates, I captured photobombed selfies of myself. I smiled while wearing my personalized decorated stole adorned with an "Oprah wasn't built in a day" button. The button represented my belief that success doesn't come overnight, but now, I was a milestone closer.

It was another moment that I sought to share with my loved ones. I had, again, reserved graduation tickets for their presence but was ultimately frustrated because they couldn't make it to the ceremony. I don't recall their reasons, but I'll never forget the feeling.

The chief executive officers of Emy's Promise, the McGuires, have also become my mentors. They purchased me an airline ticket to travel to Tallahassee to ensure I attended the ceremony. With transportation covered, I made arrangements with my colleague Naomi. She was also a social work student and graduating, so helping me wasn't an inconvenience to her schedule. She agreed to pick me up from the airport and allowed me stay at her house and celebrate with her and her family.

As I got dressed for graduation, my mind was occupied. I was focused on not forgetting anything, complying with graduations rules, and being on time. But when the speaker called my name, reality hit as the joyful screams of the previous student's family instantly dropped to a dead silence. As I prepared to walk across the stage, I couldn't help but notice there was no one in the audience to scream for me. I was always that irregular kid, forced to ignore my feelings, keep my head up, and strut like everything was okay. I couldn't stop and cry because I'd ruin the day for myself and others. So, like I'd learned to do, I kept going, making the best of the circumstances.

After the ceremony, Naomi locked arms with me as we maneuvered through the busy crowd searching for her family. I saw other students being celebrated by their families. They had banners and fan-like flyers with their faces printed on them, and they took millions of pictures. We found Naomi's family, and they did the same thing, praising her and taking millions of pictures: groups and singles, and everybody wanted their own personal photo with her. Wishing I had a family like hers, I waited on the sideline until Naomi was done and able to take photos of me. Joining them for dinner, I cringed as they showered her with heartfelt speeches and graduation gifts.

Once everyone had finished, Naomi turned to me and said, "Congratulations, Kenisha."

I smiled and replied, "Thank you," knowing she had done her best to make me feel as comfortable as possible. There was nothing she could do. She wasn't the problem. It was a deep-rooted issue: the absence of my parents and family.

Without sharing my emotions about graduation, I expressed to Mrs. McGuire that I wanted to have a celebration dinner, which they coordinated at the Capital Grille once I returned to Miami. I shared an intimate dinner in a private room with eleven guests, including the McGuires; their son, Wyatt; the Gibbs, who I had met at the Emy's Promise annual fundraiser; my godbrother; Grant; my friends Tamika and Chanel; and Chanel's husband. I walked through the doors of a decorated private room at the restaurant. As I entered the room, the guests stood, issued a round of applause, and took pictures. Mrs. McGuire greeted me with a sparkly crown with GRAD imprinted on it. It matched my rose-pink dress and silver heels perfectly. I felt like Cinderella on the night of the ball. I was special. I finally felt the energy of love, genuine support, and happiness in that room.

We chatted about traveling and education, people gave heartfelt speeches, and I received gifts. Grant's gift was a new handbag, Chanel's gift was an organizer and other materials that would be useful for my career as a case manager, and the Gibbs' gift was a beautiful flower-shaped purse made with real flowers. Unfortunately, I wasn't experienced in keeping flowers alive, so they didn't live long. The McGuires' gift was hosting the amazing dinner. I thanked them all a million and two times.

Life has its way of working out, giving you exactly what you need in your life. What felt like forever had finally come to life. People were expressing their love with action and no excuses. Grant couldn't make it to the graduation due to final exams; he was a college student at the University of Southern California. But he'd asked his professor to take his last exam a day early just to attend my graduation dinner. It's true; if people want to, they will. I hadn't seen Grant since living in Nile Gardens. He and Shakira are cousins, and befriending her in high school had allowed us to cross paths and reconnect.

My relationship with the McGuires has evolved since then. I grew to be the newest member of their family. Mrs. McGuire gave me a necklace by Dogeared as an invitation to join a jewelry ritual she and her daughter practiced. Every piece of jewelry comes with a message. Mine was named Three Wishes: "Big things start with three wishes. The more you believe, the luckier you'll be, get wishing!"

I eat Thanksgiving dinner with them every year. It's the only day of the year I get to eat one of my favorite dishes: fish dip. It's perfect with saltine crackers. They only make it once a year. I've requested it during other dinner occasions but have yet to get it, so I'm always looking forward to celebrating the holiday. Every year, they take a two-month-long vacation to an international destination, always spending time with me before departing, and they come back in time to celebrate my birthday.

I was reaping one of the lessons I'd learned from Oprah's thoughts of the day: Surround yourself with the kind of people who bring you higher.

Barriers that once hindered foster youth from pursuing graduate studies had been removed. The language of the tuition waiver became consistent between Florida statutes and the college education system. The education system now allowed youth in Florida to attend college without limitations. I took advantage of the change. I contemplated pursuing a master of social work or a master of public administration degree. After researching both career paths, I decided I'd had enough of learning about client contact in a hypothetical sense and chose to pursue public administration. I was interested in learning about policies and management and thought it would be a better route to the next level of reaching my goals. I wanted to remain a Seminole, but FIU had a good program and a sweet deal. With a GPA of at least 3.5, which I had earned, I could be exempt from taking the graduate record examination (GRE). I applied to FIU and was accepted into graduate school. My mind and heart were blown away as I read, "This application is admitted."

I planned to work full-time as a dependency case manager while earning my degree. With my degree, I would have the educational credentials to qualify for an administrative career and be an asset in the decision-making processes, laws, programs, policies, and procedures. As a worker on the front line of child welfare, I would satisfy the experience component required by most employers.

CHAPTER NINE
Burn Out

"You pray for rain, you gotta deal with the mud too. That's a part of it."
- Denzel Washington

The field of child welfare is an overwhelming beast. I spent two years, eight months, and ten days on the frontline getting an in-depth view of the system. I've been assigned to a countless number of cases resulting in reunification, permanent guardianship, TPR, youth aging out, and adoption. I built long-term relationships with colleagues despite some of our different perspectives as professionals. I've gathered enough insight to make an educated guess about what may have happened to my family and me. As complex as I expected the answer to be, it boiled down to something simple: Your experience depends on who your case is assigned to—the case manager, guardian ad litem, judge, attorney, foster parents, service providers, and anyone else who may be an active participant. And, of course, one's determination to build resilience and improve their situation are also factors.

Considering research, my foster care file, what I know about my parents, and the changes in laws and how the system operates and has been operating since 1996, I believe my family suffered from the ripple effect of underpaid, overworked and stressed case managers who produced poor quality work. Case managers who had worked during that era expressed to me that they were assigned at least sixty children, and the pay wasn't worth the stress, so, without notice, most never returned to work the next day, and others tried staying afloat. Case managers were quitting as quickly as they were hired. I assume our case file was among those lost in the shuffle, resulting in poor supervision, my mom never receiving the intervention services she needed to re-strengthen our family and me falling through the cracks of the system.

By the time I was a teenager, however, my case suffered from bad laws, lack of legal representation, overworked case managers, and caregivers who weren't willing to go the extra mile.

While reviewing my file, I noticed a familiar name. Surprisingly, it was someone whom I had worked in the field with. I was unsure of her role in my case, but per the document, she was assigned to the investigation unit that had investigated the case when I was sexually assaulted. I couldn't help but think about the person I'd met, her snobby attitude and the way she handled the case decisions. She walked around the office high and mighty like she knew everything, never made mistakes, and couldn't be told anything. She'd forgotten that the smartest people are lifetime learners. She was a veteran in the field, but she wasn't perfect. I only imagined the kind of person she'd been while working on my case. Being so fast, trying to just get the job done, she'd failed to notice the facts. I wasn't safe and was left to experience more trauma while she moved on with her life. I don't think she recognized me when we met. If she did, she never mentioned it. Maybe my case wasn't her full responsibility, but because her name is documented, I know she played a part in its negligence.

...

It's a process to become a certified case manager. First, I was required to complete three months of training and pass an exam issued by the Florida Certification Board before I could be an official dependency case manager and have cases assigned to me. The position was contingent on my passing the test. If I failed the first attempt, I could retake it; however, if I failed again, the agency would have to let me go for not meeting the stipulations of employment. Since I had completed an internship, I was ahead of the game. Training was a breeze. I passed the exam on the first attempt and was eager to start working.

The training course had two settings: the classroom and the field. The incorporation of field days was intended to allow trainees to gain on-the-job experience. Trainees were given a checklist and expected to complete each task alongside a case manager. These tasks included going on a home visit, reviewing a judicial review, a case plan, completing a service referral, and documenting a case note into Florida Safe Families Network. The challenge was to find a case manager who was doing those tasks on that specific day. If not, we wouldn't get that experience while in training.

Training does not prepare a person to be an equipped dependency case manager. During training, we watched videos about abused and neglected children and typical topics we may have seen or heard about. We read related content, completed worksheets and activities, and had discussions about policies and procedures based on Florida statutes. We identified safety threats and learned how to engage a client and make recommendations such as implementing an in-home safety plan[1] or removing the child.

The majority of training was spent covering what happens when a case is on the investigation level, which is the job of the child protective investigator. Out of three months, less than three days included guidance about providing ongoing case management services, which was the case manager's responsibility. Ongoing investigation is important. During home visits or any interaction with a client, case managers should always be assessing for danger; however, it's not the full scope of the job we're expected to do. Training only gave us an idea of the job, simply a textbook version of child welfare. Most will agree that case management is a learn-as-you-go job. I learned how to complete a task when it was time to do it.

A social work professor from Florida State University came to visit our training class as a guest speaker. She was pitching a five-year state-wide study, the Florida Study of Professionals for Safe Families, which focused on the job of case managers and child protective investigators throughout the State of Florida. The purpose of the study was to compile never-before collected data to understand the complexity of both positions and bring awareness to the

---

1   Safety Plan - a personalized, practical **plan** that can help you avoid dangerous situations and know the best way to react when you are in danger.

high turnover rate.

Catching us fresh during training was a brilliant idea because we weren't yet seasoned. The survey would follow us throughout our career. Even if workers resigned, she required that they still complete the survey. As an incentive, she offered gift cards in exchange for participation, so I signed up and committed to completing the survey every six months when a new one was sent. Receiving the survey results helped me gain insight, compare the findings to my own experience, and review recommendations for improvement as well.

The first survey findings concluded that child protection investigators and case managers felt unprepared for work and experienced quick transitions into complex caseloads. Workers voiced concerns about the disconnect between training content and agency procedures and protocol. Workers found training content to be informative but difficult to apply in real situations. Additionally, workers felt they did not have enough shadowing opportunities to prepare them for the realities of the job. Once on the job, many workers agreed that caseloads were higher than expected, and they felt like asking clarifying questions about completing job responsibilities was a burden on their colleagues.

At BRC, immediately out of training, for a thirty-day period, case managers were assigned a maximum of ten children. It was supposed to be a grace period, but in this field, a lot can happen in thirty days. After thirty days, ready or not, the caseload increased to capacity, depending on the demand. Only the strong would survive. I was amazed that a senior case manager had projected that I wouldn't last on the job. I planned to prove him wrong. This was something I really wanted to do despite what any study or person had to say.

After passing the test, I had to complete additional training, a nine-day safety methodology training to learn the new child welfare practice model being utilized in Florida. And I had to balance an eight-hour training day with ten children including parents, foster parents, service providers, guardians, GAL's, relatives, half-siblings, schools, judges, attorneys, and anybody else who was a party of the case. The cases I received were transferred from other units and had been worked on by previous workers. It was now my responsibility to tend to their needs and finish the job. While in training, I was still responsible for ensuring all cases' needs were met: home visits, court documents, transportation, case notes, referrals, reports, supervised visitation, and appointments to therapy, the doctor, and the dentist. A few case managers and I thought it was a bit extreme for them to expect us to spend eight hours in training then work after 5 p.m. But I knew this was the nature of the job, so I did what I had to do. After training, I proudly told my colleagues, "I'll see y'all tomorrow" because I had to do a home visit or whatever other task I needed to complete. In return, they gave me strange looks and laughed at my jolliness. I was just happy to have achieved my goal of becoming a case manager in child welfare, earning a salary, and losing my eligibility to receive food stamps.

My thirty-day grace period expired, and I received my first set of fully loaded cases. I don't remember the exact number of clients I had, but I'm sure it was around twenty-five. Out of this batch, probably two months later, I closed my first dependency case. The mother had spent the last few years incarcerated, and she was unable to comply with court-ordered tasks included in the case plan like parenting, gaining employment and housing, and demonstrating the ability to keep her children safe. Her release date from jail was approaching, but time was not on her side. She had exceeded the twelve-month out-of-home-care rule per Florida Statute 39.8055, which legally gives the State the right to file a petition for termination of parental rights. Rather than prolonging permanency and being invasive, I recommended that the courts close the case in permanent guardianship with the children in the care and custody of the maternal grandmother, with whom they resided.

Before the courts accepted the goal and ruled to close the case, I advocated to provide the family with bunk beds to ensure the children had appropriate sleeping arrangements. I wasn't sure why that hadn't been done before I'd received the case. It's the first task that must be completed after ensuring the children are safe. And upon being released from jail, the mother was to be provided with service referrals to comply with her case plan. The mother would live with and co-parent with her mother while caring for her children and completing court-ordered services. It can be tough to transition back into society from jail, so with this option, she was relieved of time constraints and had the option to petition the courts to regain custody of her children. The supervision of the State was no longer needed, the children were safe with a relative and their mother, services were in place, and the family was working together as a support system. Even if this plan didn't work, the children could rely on their primary caregiver, their grandmother.

On the day of the court hearing, before the judge, the grandmother delivered a heartfelt speech, expressing her gratitude for my service. Having experienced several case managers before me, she noted that I was attentive to her family's needs, knowledgeable, dependable, and informative. Known to be the toughest dependency judge in Miami, Judge Benson acknowledged the work I had done with the family. She even went further to advise the administrators at the agency of what had occurred in court. When I arrived back at the office, I was acknowledged for my work as well. I smiled and patted myself on the back. I was proud of myself for helping others as I had intended to do.

Court wasn't always that simple. Judges didn't always agree, sometimes ruling against my professional recommendation and making one of their own. Forcing me with or without the family to accept the challenge to rethink a strategic plan to reach the goals of the case. It wasn't always easy.

The research professor released the second survey. The findings concluded that out of the 235 workers who had completed the survey, 18 percent left their agencies within the first six months. The workers who had resigned were older and had prior experience in the field, more than those who stayed on the job. The two groups had no difference in coping strategies, satisfaction with pay and benefits, support received from supervisors and coworkers, or work experience. However, there was a significant difference in transition experiences between early leavers and workers who remained on the job. Workers who left hadn't received mentoring when starting their caseload responsibilities. In the first week of casework, caseload sizes ranged from zero cases assigned to twenty-seven cases. Early leavers reported a higher initial caseload than those who remained on the job. Workers who resigned also expressed discrepancies between content provided in training and agency practices, making it challenging to complete the job.

During the first year in case management, I felt the pressure and was ready to submit my resignation letter. I learned not every client would be receptive to good customer service and some would accuse me of being inexperienced based on my physical appearance. I do look young. Professionals lost sight of their roles in the process, demands of the job were overbearing and nearly impossible to complete without delays, judges would not always rule in your favor, and administrators were sometimes insensitive and appeared to only care about numbers and meeting outcomes.

During an in-home assessment[2] for a Caucasian family, the color of my skin triggered a problem. It was a new case. I was the assigned case manager and aimed to kill two birds with one stone: complete the required home study and build a rapport with the family. A home study can feel invasive to the family, as I must evaluate the entire house: the kitchen, cabinets, bedrooms, bathrooms, closets, and every other room and square foot that makes up a home. I needed to know if they had firearms, medicine, or alcohol, and if so, where they were stored. I had to see it. I needed copies of their government-issued ID's, benefits statements, social security cards, bills, proofs of income, medical records, doctor contact information, and two people who could speak on their behalf, things that most people keep private. I needed to take pictures to support my observations. I get that it's invasive. I tried to make the process easy by making small talk. But I still had to do my job to make the proper recommendation. However, the mother used it as ammunition to accuse me of being a potential thief. She believed I would steal from her home. She called the agency to complain, using racial slurs, which led the agency to recuse me from the case and

---

2 **In-home assessment** — an evaluation of the home and life of parents whose children will remain in their care during a dependency case

replace me with a white case manager.

I was doing my best. I never missed a deadline because I was daydreaming, being lazy, or lacked organization and time management skills. I was busy tending to the needs of clients, which didn't always coincide with the scheduled time frame. At one point, I had three demanding cases, and balancing their needs was driving me to insanity.

The first case was a troubled child who was in and out of home care and prescribed psychotropic medication to manage behavior that the foster parents described as uncontrollable, devilish acts. I had never witnessed this behavior; she was always an imperfect angel in my presence. She'd experienced three placement disruptions since being on my caseload, subjecting me to constant phone calls from complaining foster parents and long drives back and forth from the north side of Miami to the down south area to transport her to the next destination. As I explored ways to stabilize the placements, the foster parents were not willing to compromise; they wanted her out of their home expeditiously.

In one placement, she was assigned a one-on-one specialized behavioral aide. The one-on-one accompanied the child all day, redirecting her behavior. She hated it, so the aide was continuously replaced. On occasions, I sat and read with her to keep her calm until she fell asleep. I tried telling her that one of the behavioral aides was my friend, which slightly changed her attitude, but for her to remain calm, she still required my presence. When I attempted to walk away, she screamed, "Ms. Kenisha, Ms. Kenishhaaa." I couldn't commit to doing that every day.

The second case had five children in and out of home care. The judge ordered visitation three times a week for an hour and a half. It was my responsibility to supervise the visit and transport the children due to the unavailability of support staff. The children had a serious case of lice, and the over-the-counter treatment kit was not working to remedy the issue. The children were not admitted into school until they were cleared by a doctor. And it's not like case managers have a special pass at doctors' offices. We had to wait like everyone else. Just waiting for the doctor to see the children was a full day of work. I was hesitant about allowing them inside my personal car, but I didn't have the option of having them transported by paramedics. The seats in my car were cloth, and I feared the lice could transfer to my hair. People kept telling me that my hair was coarse and African Americans couldn't get lice; however, that had not been proved as a scientific fact. I addressed these concerns with the administrator, and he said carelessly, "Send me an e-mail. I'm leaving for the day. My daughter has soccer." I thought, if he didn't care, why should I? I wanted to make it his responsibility by resigning immediately, but I didn't. I knew I still had a job to do.

The parents didn't care that I had spent all day in a doctor's office with their children. They were invited to attend but never showed. They still wanted all three of their supervised visits per week. On some occasions, they didn't show up to the visit, which led me to require them to confirm their attendance twenty-four hours in advance. I learned that technique from Chanel. If they failed to confirm, the visit was cancelled for that day. The parents didn't agree, and I received pushback from the agency, claiming we didn't have legal grounds to implement the procedure. I was frustrated as I tried exploring ways to strategically manage my day versus wasting time on the inevitable.

Tending to this case was draining my whole day, leaving me little time to adhere to other responsibilities. The case became more complex as the foster parent had her own demands and gossiped with the already difficult parents about me sharing their business when, in fact, it was my job to brief foster parents on the dynamics of a case.

The children on the third case were also in and out of home care. There was a total of four children in two different placements. The case had ordered supervised visitation three times per week as well. Again, I was responsible for supervising the visits and transporting the children due to the support staff's unavailability. The case had been open for more than one year and transferred to me from another unit, and it was under fire. The agency was issued a rule to show cause for the previous case manager's failure to ensure the children's needs were met and services were referred and/or ongoing, all of which became my immediate responsibility to resolve. On top of that, the foster parent was difficult. When asked to take the children to the dentist, she replied, "I can't.

The bus picked them up last time." The agency didn't have a bus transporting kids to the dentist. If they did in the past, it wasn't an option now.

In the midst of it all, it was still my responsibility to adhere to the needs of other cases assigned to me. While trying to manage high-priority tasks, my supervisor sent e-mails both created by her and forwarded from our unit administrator, entailing the deadlines for case documents and home visits that were approaching or past due. I understood everyone was only doing their job, but mine seemed harder. I tried explaining my reasons for incomplete work; however, my need for assistance was disregarded, and a corrective action plan was issued, warning me that I couldn't be late for future duties. I remembered a story about a guy who was fired for failing to complete tasks on time. I thought I was on the verge of losing the job I had wanted so badly, but I accepted that if it didn't work out, that was just life.

It was unfair, so I vented to Monique because I had an established relationship with her, and it warranted a meeting that included her, my unit POA, my supervisor, and me. My supervisor expressed that she felt I was rude and complained about late task completions. Again, I explained my reasons for the late assignments. I also clarified that I wasn't intentionally being rude, but if it seemed that way, it stemmed from frustration, lack of support, and unrealistic expectations. I also thought it had something to do with cultural differences. I was the type to stand up for myself and voice my thoughts and opinions when I needed further clarification. I was not trying to undermine my supervisor's experience. It wasn't personal.

Even the duties I was expected to adhere to on that day were impossible to complete because time didn't permit it. I couldn't drive down south to pick up a child and make it back in time to pick up more children, supervise a visit with their parents, and drop them off. Plus, my body was exhausted. I refused to transport any child with the risk of falling asleep behind the wheel, possibly killing us both. If they couldn't understand that, maybe this job wasn't for me.

Monique instructed me to write down everything I had to do that day. With a detailed written account of my duties, she requested help from support workers and allowed me to go home and rest. I thought if it was that simple, why did I have to endure the heavy burden of stress in the first place? I had gotten a taste of why case managers quit at such an expeditious rate and how clients fell through the cracks and needs went unmet.

The group had completed another survey focusing on what specifically made cases exceptionally challenging. Three categories were identified: agency policies and procedures, case types, attributes and tasks, and client-related challenges. Workers reported high workloads with elevated time pressure, waiting for another worker to complete a task to move forward, uncertainty about case procedures and documents, and lack of support. Cases included egregious maltreatment such as sexual abuse, physical abuse with injury and death, child runaways, and complicated family dynamics. Specific tasks included transportation, visitation, child placements, safety planning, and identifying impending and present danger. Client-related challenges included difficulty building a rapport due to homelessness, incarceration, and out of town placements. Also, working with clients that were racist, lacked an understanding of boundaries, or were combative.

On top of the stressors of the job duties, it was even more frustrating to not be automatically compensated for becoming a certified case manager as promised during the hiring process. Living off a starting salary of $36,000, I had patiently waited for the time to qualify for a pay raise. I was told that once I became a certified case manager, my salary would increase to $40,000, but that must have been a gimmick the agency used to reel in new employees. Agencies were almost always understaffed and wasted excessive money on training by doing a poor job selecting the right candidates, often choosing seat fillers that quit before we could blink our eyes. Somebody had to be present to receive case assignments because they didn't stop coming, even if there weren't enough case managers to properly manage them. It seemed they sold false hopes then changed their words once it was time to act on their promises.

After completing a minimum of six months of fieldwork and an application explaining that I had gained education, training, and experience while on the job, as instructed, I hand-delivered my certification to the human resource manager. I expected to be compensated. Instead, I was told, "I never said that." It felt like a slap in the face. She had said the same to the other case managers as well, so there was a lot of talk and complaining in the office. But I wasn't willing to just talk about it. A twelve-hour day at work was common, and incomplete tasks were unacceptable. I had to budget accordingly due to spending two months' worth of mileage and parking and toll expenses before being reimbursed. I expected to be compensated accordingly. As low as their retention rate was, I thought they would try to retain the employees who were willing to do the work. The last thing I had on my mind was having to debate my salary. Immediately, I requested a meeting with the Chief Operations Officer to demand what was promised to me. Maybe she thought I would be like others and leave the issue alone because she dragged her feet. She said she would look into it and took a vacation without getting back with me or solving the problem. I followed up with the person she'd left in charge during her absence. I don't remember how long it took, but, eventually, the issue was addressed. One day, when I arrived at work, there was a paper face down on my desk. When I flipped it over, I saw that it was a notice of my salary increase. I was satisfied, but the situation did leave me with a bad notion about my colleagues.

Even Obama thought we should be paid more money. He proposed legislation that would force employers to reconsider the wages they were paying professionals. Those that worked more than forty hours in a given week and earned less than $47,476 a year should be compensated and paid time in a half. I was excited for a minute. This bill would have benefited me financially. After working forty hours, with all my overtime, I was earning less than half of my promised hourly wage. This bill was intended to change that. Unfortunately, a federal judge blocked the bill in the favor of employers.

The self-help habits I had adopted vanished. I began to suffer from hair loss in the center of my head. I didn't have time or energy to tend to my own physical and mental well-being while trying to maintain this job. Stress was attacking me from every angle. Even worse, the agency didn't offer therapeutic services to employees, which was insane based on the traumatic information we consumed daily. I was drowning and putting clients' needs before myself to ensure I met deadlines. I even had to pay an additional $1,050 to my orthodontist because I kept rescheduling appointments and exceeding my treatment plan for my braces. This was my breaking point.

Still, I reminded myself why I had started this career, and I kept trying my best and improving as I gained more experience in the field. Eventually, I learned how to do the job without being issued a corrective action plan. It was still stressful at times but manageable. I became immune to the nature of the job. I learned to be an efficient case manager, which meant setting boundaries and being innovative while planning my exit.

As a boundary, I was not willing to be assigned on-call duties for the entire agency. The agency selected one case manager to work on-call for one full week. On-call usually started at 7 p.m. and ended the next morning. In addition to the regular workload, the on-call case manager was also responsible for the immediate tasks of other case managers and new case assignments that may occur overnight. I didn't understand the concept of on-call. We were expected to work twenty-four hours a day for seven days in a row. When were we supposed to rest? Working overnight was not my forte. And considering the pressure it would put on my physical and mental health, I wasn't willing to take the risk.

One week when I was assigned on-call, I was suffering from the pains of my erupting wisdom teeth, which needed to be removed. To ease the pain until I was able to see a surgeon, my dentist gave me a prescription and note to stay home due to the side effects of the pain pills. But still, a worker from the agency called me to do on-call assignments. I told her I wasn't at work and I was taking pain medication, so I was unable to do it. She disregarded my physical condition and repeated that it was my assigned week. After battling with the agency about it, they figured it out. Thereafter, I found a case manager who wanted the extra cash, and I always gave him my shift. I recommended the agency hire an on-call unit. They never did.

I found my niche. To manage my time, I avoided traffic by visiting clients down south early in the morning or on weekends. I used supervised visitation or court hearings to document bio-parent visits.[3] I spent more time with misbehaving children like taking girls to get their nails done to get them to open up. It helped to improve their behavior. They didn't become perfect children, but it was a start. I used personal dollars for these activities. I completed home visits in the same vicinity on the same day. I continuously requested assistance from support workers with the hopes that one day there just may be an opening. It worked sometimes. I connected parents to outside resources, not focusing only on case plan tasks and events conducted by the agency. For instance, one of my classmates from high school took families grocery shopping, so I recommended one of my most difficult parents to benefit from this resource. It showed that although we'd had challenges, it wasn't personal on my behalf, and I was there to help.

These strategies helped to free up days during the week, allotting me time to strengthen client relationships; take children to appointments; complete required case documents; attend court hearings, mandatory meetings, and trainings; and go home on time more than once a week. But even though I had found my niche, I was still planning my exit. Even when implementing these strategies, I still had early mornings, late nights, and stressful moments.

I saw myself in a client named Heidi. She was an undocumented immigrant child under the supervision of the State due to abandonment by her parents, who had sent her to America to escape the dangers of their home country. She was undergoing the process of becoming a citizen, which takes years to complete with no specific time frame. The climate of immigration was changing at the time, making the timing even worse. I had a few other cases like this, so I was familiar with the immigration process. It can take a number of years to complete the process to become a citizen. I don't remember which step, but applicants had to be at a specific step in the process before the cabinet change, or it was going to take even longer to become a citizen.

Heidi was in relative care living with her big sister, Katie. She was a

---

3   **Bio-parent visit** — a meeting to discuss the status of the case and progress in services and assess for further needs with biological parents. It must be completed every twenty-five days.

senior in high school and pressured to contribute financially to the household. At a home visit, she inquired about independent living. A friend had told her about it, but I had to tell her she didn't qualify for the stipend or any post-eighteen services because she wasn't a citizen.

I remember the day she told me, "I have a job at a café." But I also can't forget the moment she said, "I had to quit because of ICE. I don't want to get deported."

Her sister complained about taking Heidi to appointments (which she never did), and she didn't like Heidi hanging with friends and not working, disregarding the country's manhunt for non-citizens. Katie had children of her own and had migrated to the States as well. I tried compromising with her, but she never came around and still demanded money, threatening to kick Heidi out if she couldn't contribute.

I got pushback at first due to eligibility requirements, so I was instructed to research possible shelters Heidi could go to if she was kicked out of the home. We were a system that gave children referrals to homeless shelters. What level of stability or permanency was she granted? I couldn't live with myself, knowing I had visited this young lady every month, asked her to be open with me, and then handed her a list of homeless shelters. The most difficult part was that most shelters don't accept non-citizens. What good was the system doing for her? I couldn't be another case worker who watched the calendar and didn't go the extra mile. If all failed, at least I could live with the fact I had tried.

With the support of a written report from Heidi's therapist, I advocated for Heidi before the general magistrate, explaining that I understood the eligibility requirements; however, I had a terrified child and a demanding caregiver who was vocal about her wants and the consequences. She didn't wish to care for the child, and once she turned eighteen, it was bound to get worse. Heidi would be subjected to homelessness and possible deportation, but we could change that by bringing her into licensed care. The GM had a heart that day; she ordered to extend jurisdiction and placed Heidi into licensed care a few weeks before her eighteenth birthday. She transitioned into a foster home, reaped the benefits of extended foster care, and scheduled her first meeting with the independent living team.

I reminisced on the moment I had stood before a judge with the same problem. Shedding a tear, I thought, *Do the rules apply only when we want them to?* But that day was brighter. Everything happens for a reason. The judge had denied me because God needed me to understand that struggle. I had endured that experience for Heidi. She could've easily had a different case manager who was burnt out, handed her a list of homeless shelters, and only wished her luck. But even HUD Secretary Ben Carson agrees, "Life after foster care shouldn't begin in a shelter."

Heidi hadn't been in court that day. I had told her to go to school and I would tell her what happened. I didn't want her to experience the debate, watching me plead her case or having to plead her own case and being told no by the people she'd expected to care for her. I had braced myself to deliver bad news if I had to, but life had something better in mind. This time, I had good news. Over time, I learned there's always something that can be done.

I read an article on LinkedIn stating that maybe society has it wrong. The article referenced one foster parent expressing frustrations about the stigma placed on them. The writer emphasized that the media focuses only on the bad that happens in foster care and should turn their attention to the good. The foster parent highlighted how much she loved and cared for children that entered her home, neglecting the fact that she doesn't account for everyone. I commented on the post. I disclosed that I had worn different hats in my experience with the child welfare system that had shaped my perspective. I recommended that foster parents of this kind should be role models for others. And if the media focused only on the good, it would be portraying a false narrative about the system and the experiences of those it encounters. I do believe the media should take more of a balanced approach to help impact change. I couldn't help but ponder on my own experience with foster parents. Like any other field, there's good and there's some bad.

I have met foster parents like the one described in the article. I've managed to maintain a relationship with one of them outside of fostering.

Even after I no longer worked for the agency, she decided to adopt a child and invited me to attend the adoption, so I have seen the good the woman in the article spoke about. I've encountered foster parents who follow the quality parenting initiative (QPI), an approach focusing on excellent parenting for all children in the system. It's a partnership between biological parents, foster parents, relatives, non-relatives, and agency staff. Some foster parents accepted children into their homes, treated them as their own, took them along on family trips, allowed in-home therapeutic services, transported them to all appointments, submitted supporting documentation, placed the records in the child resource record, made arrangements for transportation to and from school, and were willing to co-parent with the biological parents. This was a big help while balancing a caseload that included a limited supply of support workers, cooperative parents, fictive kin, and foster parents. Some foster parents refused to do any of the above and acted as if their home was only for shelter purposes, at times making it my responsibility to take a child to appointments, ensure a child made it to and from school, and return the child home at a time specified by the foster parent. In the meantime, the child would sit with me at the agency, which sometimes hindered me from completing other duties. They requested respite care when going on family vacations, subjecting the child to living with yet another unfamiliar person. They constantly threatened to have the child removed for reasons like having an attitude, eating too much, urinating in bed, or feeding their dog peanut butter. Or they'd demand more money from the lead agency to care for the child.

When a foster parent fails to co-parent, it's difficult on us all, including the child. If a child is having a hard time adjusting to being removed and placed into foster care with stipulations of supervised visitation, the foster parent could allow the child to call the biological parent with the phone on speaker for comfort. Countless times, I've conducted three-way calls at night for that reason. So when the foster parent called to complain about the child's behavior, I would politely explain, "It's probably because of your behavior toward them, your unwillingness to interact with their parent and what they may have overheard you say about their parent, criticizing their parenting style, financial abilities, or whether they care."

Whatever the foster parent chooses not to do becomes the case manager's responsibility. The agency does have procedures for the case manager to request a meeting to discuss difficulties they're experiencing with a foster parent, which I have utilized on several occasions. But they have not all ended in my favor.

One time, a foster parent dictated when I could enter her home, even though I was supposed to have access to her house at any time and was mandated by law to conduct unannounced visits. She triggered my curiosity. I wanted to know what foster parents were learning in training to make her think this was acceptable. I had just been assigned a transferred case because the previous case manager had quit abruptly. The visit was due and had to be completed immediately. She complained that my emergency was not hers, which I understood; however, the visit still had to be done. I explained to her this would be the first and last time, and in the future, I would be sure to schedule home visits in advance. She still complained, and I had to include a supervisor to resolve the matter. We agreed on 6 p.m. I didn't want any more issues, so I arrived at her house early. I knocked on her door at 5:59 p.m., and she refused to open it. She left me outside because the children's therapist was inside, reasoning that both of us inside the house would overwhelm the children. She was trying to teach them her idea of structure. I thought about contacting the police because I didn't know what was happening inside the house, but when I consulted with my supervisor, she told me to just wait. Waiting delayed other scheduled home visits for that day, and I had to listen to those clients complain as well. It was about 7:20 p.m. when she finally opened the door. My day didn't end until about 10 p.m., including time allotted for driving.

In some cases, the foster parents were allowed to cherry-pick through children based on which agency they were from. The most disheartening situation I had ever seen occurred when I was taking a child to a potential foster placement to meet the family. We talked for hours, discussing the placement structure, the potential bedroom, daily activities, and school, and we toured the house. The child admired the family's energy and how bright and clean the home was. I wished to have met a family like this one as a child. But the conversation took a turn. The foster parent refused the child due to a strained relationship with the agency. Hoping to find a resolution, I asked, "What is the problem?"

"The agency doesn't reimburse my money in a timely fashion. We have had disputes about various topics," she said, not fully getting into the details. And she said she had been lied to.

I understood her frustrations, but still, I tried to tell her that the child and I shouldn't be held accountable due to other employees' past behavior. "I can't speak for them or the agency, but I can establish an agreement between you and me to care for this child," I offered.

Her distaste for the agency prevented us from reaching a common ground, and just like that, she decided the child couldn't be placed with her.

I wondered if the placement specialist had told her which agency we were with. Child placements are the responsibility of the lead agency, and they were known for leaving out pertinent information when trying to place children. But if she did know, why waste our time? After the child had gotten a whiff of a potential placement, she thought she had found a new home, but I had to tell her it wouldn't be. Over fried shrimp, chicken wings, and fries at Hooters, a place she had never been, I explained that it wasn't her fault, that she hadn't said or done anything wrong.

There are zero consequences for this kind of behavior. A person like me could never become immune to this atmosphere, remembering how I felt when I was a child in the same position. I had previously spent Saturdays attending trainings to share my experiences with GAL's and having open discussions on how to be an asset to a child's life. I wished I'd had one of my own, but it seemed that I had fooled myself because working with them was sometimes challenging. Some GAL's failed to do their job and were not active participants on the case. They would call me a day before the court hearing, sometimes after hours, hoping I answered the phone to collect information to complete their report. Well, that's not sufficient if you're not active and making recommendations based on your own observations. The upsetting part was when the case was under control and a GAL had the audacity to make an unnecessary recommendation such as completion of another service or they disagreed with closing the case for some unforeseen reason. At those times, our opinions differed so much that it felt like we were on a battlefield. It seemed their voice held more weight in the courtroom than mine. The role of a GAL is important, but having one that doesn't understand their role can be detrimental to the livelihood of the client. We are here to help families. Child welfare is not a punitive system; it's not as if people are sentenced to jail for making mistakes. That's not how it goes.

A GAL's egregious behavior and unreasonable recommendations forced me to disclose that I had aged out of foster care, and I didn't want to see a child age out. He thought differently because he confused poverty with neglect, was new to the system and had no knowledge of the barriers youth face when aging out. The child had been diagnosed with a serious medical condition and was behind in school, resistant to therapy, rude, and hard to place into a foster home. There was no way I was going to recommend that her case goal be changed to APPLA when it didn't need to be; she had a present mother.

We should not recommend TPR because a parent is not living according to our ideals. She had been reunified with her children, she had overcome a drug addiction, and social security was her only income, so she could meet her children's basic needs. No, she couldn't afford to take them to Disney World, but that didn't make her a bad parent. She was doing her best. The GAL was unsatisfied with her best. The pressure the GAL was putting on this mother led her attorney to address the courts to report his behavior. He even got on my nerves at times, filing unnecessary petitions in court and calling me to tell me she wasn't home during unannounced visits. I think she lost herself and set aside her idea of parenting while trying to please him and convince him to recommend closing her case. When she realized she couldn't, she relapsed and lost hope—and, eventually, custody of her children.

The day of the TPR hearing, she didn't show up to court. After I'd left the agency, her attorney relayed to me that, during meetings, she would say, "Ms. Kenisha always fought for me."

Before I transitioned into my new position, she had expressed to me that she did not want her case to be assigned to the case manager it was being transferred to. She had worked with him in the past and was not fond of his services. I communicated her concerns to my supervisor. I was told she had to accept what was available. Her concerns and wishes were ignored. She was left in a position feeling she had no power in her life and everyone on her case only penalized her for past mistakes.

I disliked receiving transferred cases. It was likely that the previous worker had left the case in total disarray, leaving me to clean up the mess. I started to understand the cases were dependent on who it was assigned to. For one case, during the case staffing, the previous worker explained that the case was headed into TPR. When I asked her reasoning, she explained that the children's behavior was out of control, and the mother had failed to address and correct their behavior. She also noted that the mother suffered from physical and mental health diagnoses, highlighting that she was unable to articulate the medication the doctor had prescribed.

Instead of submitting a request for assistance, I chose to supervise the family myself to render my own observations. During the first supervised visit, I didn't get the same impression as the previous case manager. The mother had arrived on time to the visit, greeted her children, brought food and snacks, prepared the food, and cleaned up. The family watched a movie, and the children were well behaved. Other visitation sessions were interactive as the mother assisted her children with completing homework assignments and redirected their behavior when necessary. The mother attended the children's appointments and engaged with the foster parents regarding the children's well-being and necessities. While the previous case manager had deemed the family dysfunctional, I thought otherwise.

Listening to my intuition and standing firm with my recommendation, I took a few steps to reunify the family. As I began the home study process, I noticed a trend in the mother's light bill. Some time ago, she had fallen behind and had not been able to catch up on the balance. She paid the bill to keep the lights on in the house, but the balance still followed her. Knowing how particular the assigned Quality Assurance Specialist could be when reviewing documents, to avoid pushback and delaying reunification, I referred the mother to the Low-Income Home Energy Assistance Program (LIHEAP). LIHEAP is a federally-funded program that helps low-income households with their energy bills. Unfortunately, LIHEAP was not helpful as they did not have any funding available at the time. I paid the balance with my own money, giving the mother a clean start on the next month's bill. While I had avoided one possible barrier, other stipulations by other professionals sparked a debate but ended in a compromise to not delay reunification.

The GAL requested that the mother walk the children to and from school a block away from the home every day. They did have to cross a main road on their walk to school; however, having once lived in that neighborhood, I knew that on every corner there were crossing guards that the school district employed to ensure the children's safety. There was no legitimate reason that walking to school would be a safety threat to the children's well-being. Walking with her children to school could be a protective action, but it should not have been a condition that determined reunification, specifically because an unkempt house was what had brought the family before the Department. Based on my observations, it was an issue the mother could have remedied without removal of the children. But I wasn't the CPI on the case, so there we were. Furthermore, the mother had demonstrated protective capacities by contacting law enforcement to arrest the children's father for violating an effective restraining order due to domestic violence. Even with that evidence, the GAL still wanted the mother to walk with the children. Sometimes I had to compromise to come to a resolution, so I agreed to the stipulation. The children returned to the care and custody of their mother that day.

...

I needed a break. Life as a case manager consumed me. My caseload was fluctuating from twenty-two to more than thirty children. Even when I did have time for myself, I didn't have energy. I don't know how I managed to incorporate graduate school into my life. When the agency reopened a home study unit, I applied. The last time the position was open, I didn't get it because I didn't have enough experience in case management. For sure, this time, I had a chance and got the position. As a home study case manager, I had a caseload of a maximum of five children, sometimes six, with a maximum of seven home studies to assess potential child placements. The position wasn't an advancement; it was a lateral move and a breath of fresh air.

One case that stood out to me involved an aunt trying to gain custody of her nephews, but she faced barriers due to a past issue with DCF. She had relinquished her parental rights when her son was seventeen years of age. When this information was presented to the courts, the aunt was automatically denied as a placement option. I don't know what happened to cause her case to be set for further review, but that was how I received it. This was a tough decision.

How could I assess the option and ensure she would provide a safe, stable, long-term placement if necessary? I initiated the home study process and began to have conversations with the prospective caregiver. She was forthcoming with information and articulated the details of her past and current life circumstances. She provided the contact information for her son, whom I interviewed separately to learn about his relationship with his mother. Despite their past, he had nothing but good things to say. Most important, she provided pictures and videos of her and her nephew to show they had an established bond. The photos showed them gardening, doing homework, and playing outside. Her home was already prepared for the children as they had their own rooms, appropriate beds, and space for their belongings.

My assessment determined the placement was appropriate for the children. However, I received pushback from my POA. The agency could not submit an approved home study due to the caregiver's history with the Department. I disagreed and believed it would be a healthy and stable placement with a relative. I argued, why waste my time doing this assessment if you all knew this placement was going to be denied? Also, that I would do a poor job if I were called to defend a denial in court. The children shouldn't have been subjected to living with a stranger when a willing and able relative was available. Professional recommendations should be based on current assessments. No, we shouldn't disregard a person's past. Some behaviors are, lawfully, automatic disqualifiers, as they should be. But if the potential caregiver has demonstrated that they've learned from past behavior, as a system, we should adhere to that.

After all the hoopla, both my supervisor and administrator decided to sign off on my recommendation to submit to the courts for a final decision. It was another one of my finer moments of using my voice.

...

Continuing to work in the field, I began to feel the advocacy work that I had done was not nearly enough to change the system. I had only scratched the surface. Being in the thick of it, I saw other issues occurring before children aged out of the foster care system that required attention. I applied a theory about fish, the lake, and groundwater. The theory challenges whether systems are addressing social issues by helping the fish in the lake, or if the issue is the lake causing harm to the fish. Or is the deeply rooted problem stemming from the groundwater, a problem so deep that even if we helped a set of fish by cleansing the water, the next set would still experience the same problem. I was a fish joining the lake and couldn't make a difference because the problem was deeper than what I'd thought. My advocacy work was only helping the fish, not fixing the lake or addressing the groundwater issues: poverty; housing; mental, physical, and emotional health; employment; education; substance abuse; access to quality therapeutic services; and a burdened workforce.

It dawned on me that no matter how often advocates went to Tallahassee to advocate for legislative changes, it did no good if agencies that were required to implement policies and services were understaffed and the employees were overworked, stressed, and underpaid with a lack of motivation to do the job. I've heard the saying, "Proper preparation prevents piss poor performance." We can improve the statutes that govern the child welfare system and the livelihood of children and families a million times, but if the frontline is not producing quality work, children and families will continue to suffer at the hands of the system. That goes across different spectrums of the frontline. All services are referred out to different human service agencies that are experiencing the same high turnover rate.

If a client is referred to individual therapy, but the agency has a shortage on therapists, it leads to a number of issues: The client's intake assessment and the timeliness of services will be delayed, a therapist can have a high caseload, which is ineffective for the client, and if a therapist quits, the client will be subjected to starting the therapeutic process over because they won't have a rapport with the new therapist. The therapist would have to build a rapport with the client to make appropriate recommendations, ultimately delaying permanency and the reunification of families. The cycle continues.

...

The job was interesting. Every day was different, and every case was unique. I could never be sure what to expect, and that's what I liked about it, but my love for it had died. Things needed to change. I had resignation on my mind. Although my job was something I once enjoyed, I had reached a point where I had mixed feelings. I started to become desensitized, frustrated in other instances because some families didn't need intervention, but we were forced to service or prolong their cases. And a part of me just outgrew it. I was ready for advancement to the next level. There was no room for growth within the agency. I didn't have interest in becoming a case manager supervisor. I was interested in an administrative role in policy, programs, and procedures to improve system operations, create new positions, reallocate resources, and improve the quality of members of the frontline who could benefit from improved medical benefits, incentives, better work conditions, a positive office culture, increased salaries, and a promising retirement plan. Ultimately, improving the system of care for the customers we serve.

But first, I had to earn my master's degree. I was near the end of my program. I completed the core classes and needed to locate an internship focusing on administration to meet graduation requirements. I spoke with Monique about interning with the agency again. I was interested in completing the internship in the independent living unit. I thought the unit could benefit from an efficient system that identified youth who were going to age out and work with them to develop life skills and a strong transition plan. This was a pivotal moment for youth, and it was careless for the independent living specialist to initiate the plan after the child turned seventeen years old, a few months before their eighteenth birthday. Sometimes just two or three months before the child's birthday, they'd tap my shoulder as I walked the office hallway to tell me they needed to meet with the child immediately to meet the required deadline, leaving me to wonder if the specialist had not just seen me, how much longer it would have taken them to appropriately schedule a meeting. The last-minute technique was an inconvenience for me, a disadvantage to the child, and a hindrance from achieving a solid transition plan. The process is weak. What if the child wants to go to college? Two to three months is not enough time to ensure everything is in place for a stress-free transition.

Resources are only beneficial to the people who know about them. If the child has limited access to the world and no one to inform them, how will they know what's available? I thought the agency could benefit from improved community relations. It dawned on me that the agency lacked partnerships with philanthropists, which was another disadvantage for youth. I did a Google search for available resources and opportunities. There are numerous organizations that does good work in the community geared toward helping underserved youth. We were always ranting about limited resources, but how much would we really have if we worked together? I had never seen e-mail blasts or pamphlets informing us about community events. I remember sending an e-mail to inform case managers that the CAP scholarship issued by the Miami Foundation was open and accepting applicants and instructed them to inform youth on their caseloads who were headed to college about it. But that was one time, and I never saw another e-mail like it.

An internship to improve these areas in the agency would have been good, but my idea was shot down. The agency had undergone budget cuts and begun eliminating positions. The lead agency was reevaluating the organization's responsibility for the independent living section. I don't know why, but it prevented me from interning there. Then I was told if I interned as a program administrator, I would have to resign because it would be a conflict of interest. I couldn't supervise my supervisor. The other downside was that I would have to work for free and, of course, I still had bills, so that wasn't the most ideal scenario.

I kept searching, reminding myself not to stress, to trust the process, and things would work out. I received an e-mail from the outreach coordinator at FIU including details about a paid internship opportunity from Broward County Board of Commissioners with the county administrator. After applying and completing three rounds of interviews, I was selected and submitted my two-week resignation to the agency. Out of my desire to advance and gain administrative experience, I had made my exit plan from case management a reality.

TESTIMONY
Dependency Case Manager[4]

As a current dependency case manager (DCM) with about three years of experience, I must say the job has its days. Out of training, the job felt like a hazing initiation as tasks were thrown at me with little to no guidance. There were days when I was ready to resign without notice immediately. But with friends, including Kenisha, already in the field, I was able to seek advice and support, even though they had caseloads of their own. Following their lead, over time, I got the gist of how to get the job done at my own pace with time management, organization, planning, and execution. So far, it's working but still has its days. I ask myself how much can I take because the job is a beast. But I take it one day at a time and do my best to take care of myself emotionally and mentally.

I am satisfied with the luxury of flexibility and limited direct supervision. I have heard stories from other case managers, so this benefit depends on the case manager and the supervisor's management style. I have found time to breathe once I've completed my tasks. Of course, I get right back to work when it's time to complete new ones.

If I had a magic wand to change one thing about the child welfare system, it would be to increase employee incentives because the high turnover causes my workload to be more challenging and almost impossible to do with no exceptions from administrators.

---

4   This is one of several testimonies received by former and current Dependency Case Managers.

CHAPTER TEN

There's Beauty in the Struggle

"God blessed me with unbelievable parents."
- Magic Johnson

During in-service training, the trainer made a statement: "Keep in mind, no matter how unfit they are to you, a child will always love and want to be with their parent." It's a true statement. No matter what happened, I wanted my parents. I wanted to experience their presence, love, and protection. That day, I was assured that my confused feelings had been normal. I had battled myself, wondering why I still wanted my parents when they continuously showed me they didn't feel the same.

That's the crazy part about this lifestyle. Time and time again, my parents proved they were unfit, but still, I tried. I thought my presence alone would change their hearts. Instead, I hurt myself more, learning that I wasn't enough to change them. People constantly made excuses for their behavior and my pain by saying, "That's still your mother" or "That's still your father." I eventually realized I'd had enough of the pain, and if I wanted to be happy and live a prosperous life, I had to let them both go. They were toxic.

My relationship with Gina was like a rollercoaster. There were times when she wasn't being forced on me, but I felt so emotionally burdened that I'd go search for my mom. I needed her.

Riding in a car down 22nd Ave., I'd look to the left and see her. One time, I had mentioned to the driver of the car, "That's my mama." Without asking, the driver turned the car around so I could see her. As we approached her, I rolled down the back window to say hi, but, with a straight face, she looked me in the eyes and repeatedly told me to leave. When I attempted to speak, she interrupted me. "Leave."

When I was nineteen, I'd catch the bus alone to a drug-infested area to find her. Some days were blank trips while others were better. I identified myself as her daughter and asked everyone I saw, "Have you seen Gina?" Some ignored me while others were nice. They knew how dangerous the neighborhood was, so they told me to wait at Homestyle, a popular restaurant in Opa-Locka. Sometimes they were able to bring her to me; other times, they claimed they couldn't find her. A part of me felt she just didn't want to see me. When I did get to see her, we'd talk, and sometimes I'd buy her a plate of food.

During one conversation, I built up the courage to ask her when she was going to come home. Her response is something I've blocked from my mind.

Randomly, one day, she called my phone asking me to bring her groceries. I called a friend for a ride and used my food stamp card to get non-perishable foods like rice, beans, bread, and canned goods, thinking I was doing something good. But she yelled at me and questioned why I didn't just bring her the money.

Frustrated with her behavior, I asked again, "When are you coming home?"

She continued her rant about money and ignored my question.

I told her to never call my phone again, realizing that wanting my mother in my life was only breaking my heart. I had to put our relationship behind me.

Going against my word, I allowed others to convince me otherwise when I knew what was best for me. When I was twenty-one, I received a call about my mother being in a coma. My boyfriend used the infamous line "That's still your mother" and persuaded me to go to the hospital against my better judgement. When we arrived at the hospital, Gina wasn't in a coma. In fact, she had physical mobility and had more than a few words to say. I was busy asking about her well-being while she fussed, reminding me that she had birthed me and I was supposed to take care of her and give her money to get her hair done and buy a cell phone. She even accused me of spending my money to take care of my boyfriend. I was over it. Angry, I told her she would never see me again. And I meant it that time. The car ride home was painful and silent. I blamed myself for allowing it to happen again. I had known better.

Years passed before another random call came about Gina—she was in the hospital again. She was in a coma and suffering from asthma. People contacted me, and I advised them to leave me out of it. I was protecting myself and had no interest in being disappointed again. For some time, Craig and Ashley had refused to speak with her, but this time, the roles had changed. Craig booked the next flight to Miami to be with her and hoped she'd leave with him to get herself together. But instead, after healing from her hospital stay, she returned to the streets.

Craig tagged Gina in a Facebook post, ranting about his disappointment, claiming that she had hurt us both, but this time, she hadn't hurt me. I had spared myself the disappointment, wishing my brother had done the same.

Eventually, her poor health got the best of her. Five years later, she was back in the hospital, and on October 31, 2016, she passed away. I was at the mall shopping when I received a call from Ashley. The medical examiner's office had contacted her letting her know Regina was dead and her body was at the morgue. She explained Gina had been in a coma for the past few months and didn't survive her health complications. All I could say was, "Okay." It was weird because a few days prior, I could have sworn I'd seen her face. She was smiling at me as I sat at the red light on State Road 9 near her hangout spot. Maybe that was her spirit saying goodbye.

I felt a sense of relief. Her passing meant only one thing: I didn't have to worry about falling victim to her calling and saying she was ready to clean up and come home only to leave again. Another part of me felt different. A part of me wanted to see her to confirm her death was real and get closure, so I went to the morgue to see her, thinking if I saw her it would be my final goodbye. The receptionist confirmed that she was there but informed me that I was unable to see her. To see her, I would have had to pay for her body to be transferred to a funeral home plus all the other expenses for a funeral.

That was the end. I would never have a chance at having a mother.

I still cry because I will never experience my mother's love, but I'm living with it.

The thing that strikes me the most is that my foster care file repeatedly states that my father's whereabouts were unknown and that he was never in my life. One time they'd found him in prison, but reunification was not an achievable goal based on his release date and my age. It's not noted in the file, but I remember taking a DNA test confirming he was my father which tells me he never signed my birth certificate. I learned through a conversation with him that the judge had granted him supervised visitation when I was five years old, a decision that he despised. John revealed that during a supervised visit, he had walked out, announcing, "No one is going to watch me while I visit my daughter! If that's the case, I'll see her when she turns eighteen." He meant that. I can count on one hand the number of times I'd seen him before turning eighteen years old—close to none.

Reconnecting with my father was our chance to make things right, a chance to have my family. I was ecstatic when Mylika, Joy, John, and I were reunited. I was eighteen, and the system wasn't there to dictate our lives. Together, we attended a family reunion, and, for the first time, I got to interact with the paternal side of my family.

I learned several things. They'd lived no more than ten blocks away from me when I lived with Grandma Rose. We lived close, and we'd see each other at the neighborhood grocery store, but when Grandma Rose told them I was John's daughter, they ignored us. Another part of the family lived on the next block. They shared an alleyway separating our backyards, but none of them cared to have a relationship with me.

I didn't know much about how jail or its pre-trial release program worked when I was arrested and charged with assault at eighteen. John did, so I went to him, happy I could turn to my father for guidance. I was released from jail and ordered to report to the pre-trial center monthly until the case was resolved. I showed him the papers, and he knew exactly what I needed to do, where to go, and what bus to catch. The reporting time was early, so early that it would still be dark outside while I waited at the bus stop. The world is crazy; I was scared to catch the bus that early in the morning by myself, I asked him to go with me so I could feel safe. I spent the night at his house, and we woke up the next morning and went to check-in at a building down the street from Turner Guilford Knight Correctional Center. But the night before had ruined the moment, causing me to feel awkward and contemplate how to proceed with pursuing the relationship. I soon learned that I can't make things right with a person who hasn't resolved the underlying issues that had damaged us in the first place.

The night before, he took me to say hi to a guy I had never met, but he claimed he dated my mom back in the day. I had never seen the guy a day in my life and didn't know how he knew me, not that it mattered to me. He confirmed that he had dated my mom, ranted about how big I had gotten, and gave me twenty dollars, of which John requested half. I was reluctant, but he argued that if it weren't for him, I would have never gotten the money. I gave it to him, and he used the money to buy drugs and used them right in front of me. I had to take myself to another room of the house.

I tried putting the thought out of my head, but the walls didn't drown out his grunts of satisfaction. The first night I spent with him, he called his friend over and they got high. He was so disrespectful. It was distasteful, and I felt he had exploited me to feed his own bad habits. I never mentioned it to him, but it's something I've kept bottled up inside. I'd lost a little hope. I kept trying, but his behavior wouldn't keep me around for much longer.

In his version of the story, he denied introducing my mother to drugs and blamed everything on her. He lacked accountability. He claimed that my mom was crazy and accused him of touching me as a little girl. I don't remember anything like that; then again, I don't recall a lot of stuff people have told me. I didn't want to victimize myself, but I also didn't know what to believe. I had never heard of the accusation and felt he was confusing me even more. I didn't want to know anymore. I just wanted him to stop, but he didn't know how. Other times, he would call, advising me to beware of what my mom was saying about him on the streets and warning me not to allow her to turn me against him. With no idea of what he was talking about, I would respond, "Bro, I don't be around you or her crackhead friends to hear anything y'all talking about." I think he was high and living in the past. He told stories about his life as a drug dealer and boasted about the money he'd earned before going to prison. But then he'd switch gears, telling me I needed to buy him T-shirts and socks.

I even tried to have a relationship with my paternal grandmother, Hattie. I'd heard stories about how Hattie didn't like my mother and how her son couldn't do any wrong in her eyes. Still, I tried, but it didn't work. Hattie couldn't stop blaming my mother and talking about how crazy she was and her accusations of my father touching me. I thought maybe Hattie had Alzheimer's, because she sounded like a broken recorder, repeating herself and bashing Gina as I tried several times to change the topic. There was no other option but to give up. I reminded her that I was her granddaughter, gave her a pocket-sized photo from my high school graduation, and walked away.

I started to pull away. John noticed the change in my behavior because he started only calling to talk to my boyfriend. He wouldn't even ask how my day was, just, "Where's your old man?" Since he wanted to talk to him rather than me, I told them to exchange numbers and talk as much as they wished, which they did. What I didn't know was that he would vent to my boyfriend behind my back as if I were the bad person in the situation. I couldn't figure out why my boyfriend always spoke like I was being unreasonable for not wanting to have a relationship with my father.

One day, he called my boyfriend's phone, and my boyfriend put him on speaker. I heard my dad saying that he and my sister, Joy had spoken about me, and they decided that I acted like they owed me something, and I only called them when I needed them. I was lost. What had led to them feeling that way? I was jealous of the bond he and Joy shared, questioning why he was able to be a father to her but not me. I felt like he had cherry-picked which child he wanted to care for. It was something he never cared to explain. Apparently, he felt he didn't owe me an explanation.

He was still using drugs, and pursuing the relationship was causing more damage than good. I had no interest in trying to rebuild a toxic relationship or using the energy to plead with people to accept my truth and validate the way I felt. Pain from the past doesn't disappear because time has passed. I had to face it to overcome it. Having my parents in my life was doing more damage than good. Mentally, I noted that I was done. If I wanted to heal from the pain, it couldn't be with them in my life.

After not speaking to John for years, the last time I saw him was at my boyfriend's mother's funeral. When I saw that he was there, I realized he was good for being supportive to everyone but me. When Gina had passed away, he didn't try to reach out to me. Yet here he was at someone else's mother's funeral.

On May 10, 2019, I had one goal. My mood, spirt, and soul were all in a high place. I was prepared to be inspired and check an item off my bucket list. Finally, I was going to hear Mrs. Michelle Obama speak in the flesh. As I sat under the hair dryer waiting for my freshly washed and styled natural hair to dry, my little sister Mylika called on FaceTime.

She started the conversation by asking, "What are you doing?" and eased into letting me know that John had transitioned.

I hung up in her face, clueless as to why she felt she needed to let me know that he'd died. My time to respond was short, I had to rationalize in the midst of a million emotions and thoughts. Mylika was persistent. She called back, and I didn't answer. Instead, I replied with an autoresponder text message: "Can I call you later?"

But she called again. I answered.

She asked, "Did you hear me?"

"I heard you say John's name, and I don't know why you would be calling me about him," I said.

"Before you see it anywhere else, I just want to tell you that John has transitioned." She said.

I played dumb and asked, "Where?"

"He is no longer with us," she explained.

I didn't really know how to respond. I felt uneasy because I didn't know what to do with the information. This was my father. Normal people felt heartache when their parents died. But I was reminded that I wasn't normal. I wished she had spared me the news because there was nothing I could do with it but feel confused and contemplate the fact I'd never had a father, and since he was dead now, I never would. Like Tupac Shakur, they'd said I was wrong and heartless, but while I was looking for a father, he was gone.

I always try to be a better big sister than what I had. Even while battling with disassociating myself from my paternal family, I had to come to terms with myself. Mylika is my baby sister, and nothing that happened was her fault. If I distanced myself from her, I'd become the same kind of person I despised. I wasn't sure how she felt about John's passing, and in an effort to be a better person, I asked, "How do you feel?"

"At peace," she said.

We sat in silence for about three minutes before ending the phone call.

I chose not to participate in either of my parents' home goings. Gina didn't have a funeral, but my family argued about it. Politely, I told them the decision was theirs to make; I didn't want anything to do with it. Despite the difference of opinions about having a funeral, Ashley and Craig decided to have her cremated. The decision was finalized based on the fact that Gina hated her sister, and no one had helped her or us when she was alive. Ironically, Shawn hated their decision, but it wasn't hers to make. She wanted to have a funeral. Gina would have turned over in her grave had Shawn been allowed to make a mockery over her deceased body.

John had a funeral, but I knew there was nothing a dead body could say to me. And at funerals, people tended to speak about only the good in people. I had a difference of opinion. I let them mourn in peace and didn't attend the service rather than upsetting myself and suffering in discomfort.

My parents' deaths were unexpected, but they were occurrences I could have lived without knowing about; they were already dead to me. I wasn't on a journey of forgiveness. I lived my life accepting that they were not a part of it. But since I do know, I feel like a weight has been lifted from my shoulders. I no longer have to worry about new traumatic experiences or them reaching out wanting to be parents and me falling into the trap and being disappointed.

Jealousy surfaced as I dwelled on the fact that my siblings had experienced our mom and dad in capacities that I hadn't. I'm the odd middle child. I wish I had memories like Ashley. She remembers Gina being like Clair Huxtable, Florida Evans, and Aunt Vivian, a strong black woman and caring mother, like the TV mothers of our culture. I cringed when Mylika expressed on social media that she was at peace knowing that John had lived his life to the fullest and included a picture of them at her birthday party. How could a person live his life to the fullest knowing he didn't care for all of his children? I felt empty. I will never have the chance to experience loving parents like my siblings had. They're gone forever. And, weirdly, the thought crossed my mind that they had died selfishly, leaving me to live with this reality for the rest of my life. It's something I continue to learn how to cope with. I don't believe it's a wound that can ever be healed.

"A thought can manifest itself into physical form."
— Lisa "Left Eye" Lopez

One of the biggest threats to reunification is housing. It's a national crisis. I've seen parents successfully complete therapeutic services according to their case plans but still risk losing their children due to the lack of affordable housing. With the clock ticking after the twelve-month permanency rule,[1] parents scramble to locate a job paying a living wage and/or affordable housing. They plead to the judge, asking if there is anything that can be done to help them get into the Section 8 housing program. But the judge informs them that nothing can be done to skip the line for housing. The State then files a TPR petition, adding to the parentless child population, putting more kids at risk of the pitfalls of foster care and life.

My curiosity was aroused. I wished the system had a pool of money and housing and employment navigators for parents who weren't a danger or threat to their children but struggled in these areas. I also wondered why it took a century for applicants of the Section 8 program to receive calls back. So, when given a writing assignment by my professor, I focused my attention on researching the housing crisis in the United States. I earned an "A," and found that the mismanagement and theft of funding for housing by private developers and public service professionals is the leading cause to the insufficient number of affordable units. One of the criminals admitted that had he not stolen the money, it could have helped ten more families. It further fueled my thirst to learn about the checks and balances and ensure this didn't happen in the future.

In an interview for an internship opportunity, I had an open dialogue with the county administrator of Broward County about myself and affordable housing and ethics. The conversation was centered around my experience and

---

1   Time is of the essence for permanency of children in the dependency system. If a parent has failed to substantially comply with a case plan to achieve reunification, then the Department has the right to file a petition for TPR.

research, landing me the position with the Community Partnership Division in the Homeless Initiative Partnership section. The internship focused on an array of administrative duties centered around funding, housing, contracts, and homeless services provided in the county.

To earn my degree, I needed to complete 300 hours in an administrative role. The internship was a one-year commitment. I completed more than enough hours, meeting graduation requirements. On the ninth of December 2018, I received my Master of Public Administration degree and a graduate certificate in human resource policy and management. Proudly, I wore my cap and gown decorated with a blue stole provided by Sew Educated to represent adults that were once in foster care who graduate.

I reflected on the things I had been through to reach this moment in life. I wanted to cry tears of joy but didn't want to smear my makeup. I stretched my eyes to keep the tears from falling, in disbelief that I was seconds away from hearing my name called to walk across the stage while my sister, niece, brother, and mentors sat in the stands supporting me. It felt like a dream, but it was my reality despite naysayers and statistics about foster youth. Proudly, I wore my cap and gown decorated with a blue stole provided by *Sew Educated* to represent foster kids who graduate. Once again, I was on the other side of the statistics. I was free of student loan debt and accomplished. That day, the game changed, and it had all started with a thought that manifested.

CHAPTER ELEVEN

Trigger Warning

"Healing begins where the wound was made."
- **Alice Walker**

"1 out of every 2 kids who age out of foster care will develop
a substance dependence."
"25% of youth experience direct effects of PTSD."
- **NFYI**

I'd spent my life surviving. I was focused solely on improving my circumstances with little room for mistakes while earning degrees, gaining financial stability, maintaining my well-being, and establishing a place to call home. In my first one-bedroom apartment, I was grateful to have my own space, a bed, and a dresser drawer filled with more than two dozen pairs of panties and bras, things I'd had to steal in the past. I'm a habitual Victoria's Secret shopper. I used to purchase new undergarments every payday. Now, I shop anytime I can catch a good sale.

I felt I had acquired everything I needed to live a happy life, but I hadn't. I felt empty and realized something important was missing. The reality I had been determined to escape had only been suppressed and had resurfaced. Lonely nights at my dinner table caused me to remember that I was missing a family.

I believed I had found a family with my most recent boyfriend, Zion. He managed to do all the right things, easing me into letting my guard down. With him, I felt lighter, cared for, protected, and loved. It was the happiest I had been in a long time. After meeting as childhood friends and reconnecting in college, our friendship transformed into a love story. After waking up beside each other every morning, traveling to school by public transportation, studying, setting goals, volunteering, and eating dinner together, I had fallen in love with my best friend. Zion had a sweet side, always boasting about how smart I was and encouraging me. Without asking, he brought me medicine when I was sick, lunch when I was hungry, and was always on time picking me up from work at 5 p.m. In his eyes, I was Superwoman. He was the only guy to have met both my mother and my father. He knew the truth about my family. He challenged my conscious behavior. Normally, I didn't make plans to celebrate my birthday. It grew to be just another day for me, but he changed that, reminding me that I was worth being celebrated. Typically, I'd go home when his family had outings. But one day, as they got dressed to attend another event, his mother questioned why I always went home when they went out. Zion joked that maybe I thought I was too good to hang out with them, which wasn't true. From that point, I went with them to almost everything. He encouraged me to spend time with his mom, so I built a bond with her. Spending time with her reminded me of my time with Auntie Mae. Together, we'd watch evening television shows, shop, get our nails done, decorate the Christmas tree, and have interpersonal conversations about any subject. At the wash house, she showed me how to wash and fold Zion's clothes. She also showed me how to cook for him because Zion is a pescatarian, and I was still eating poultry at the time. I think she was preparing me to be the perfect wife for the man of my dreams.

I felt a sense of belonging as they welcomed me into their family. I was finally in a space that I wasn't forcing myself to be a part of. I was open and comfortable with our lifestyle and daily routines, but Zion's infidelities ultimately changed everything between us. They tore us apart and placed burdens on our relationship that we have yet to overcome.

I fell into a depression. I went into a shell, following a strict routine to control my thoughts and protect my feelings. I lived by a rule: If it wasn't inside my house, I didn't need it. I didn't want to see Zion or interact with anyone who could mention him. I left my house only for school and work, which was on the same campus. I deleted all my social media accounts. For a while, I stopped listening to music to avoid relating to lyrics that could trigger what I was feeling inside. It worked momentarily.

Zion and I separated and were going through the motions of a relationship gone bad. He showed up at my job and approached me in the hallways at school, claiming he just wanted to talk. Sometimes, I ignored him. On a bad day, I exploded and responded by screaming at him with foul language, hoping he'd leave me alone. But neither stopped him. Zion's insistent behavior didn't include a clear and valid explanation as to why he'd cheated on me and ruined our relationship. It wasn't until months after we broke up that I understood our complicated situation.

One day, outside of my strict routine, due to my dryer malfunctioning, I had to go to the wash house to dry my clothes. Unfortunately, I ran into a familiar face who enlightened me about what Zion had failed to tell me: he was soon to be a father. I was devastated, and I cried the entire night. My heart stopped beating twice. I needed to be pinched, hoping to wake up from a bad dream. I was confused. The last time I had seen Zion was earlier that day. He'd shown up to my job but didn't mention anything about a child, nor had he for the past five months.

I needed to hear the truth out of Zion's mouth. I wanted him to look me in the eyes and tell me he was soon to be a father. The next day, I pulled myself together and questioned him. And like a typical guy, he placed the blame on my angry behavior for why he was unable to tell me about his son. But, overall, he was honest. We sat and talked for more than three hours. We both were vulnerable, so what started as a heated conversation transformed into a civilized one. It was the first time we talked without fussing and fighting since breaking up. That day, we agreed to be friends. Zion asked me to promise him I wouldn't hate him the next day. It was a promise I made but couldn't keep. In that moment, hearing the truth made me feel better, but it was only a temporary fix.

I loved him so much that I had erroneously rationalized that we could be cordial and friends. But this new friendship we had established was a roller coaster. It was without boundaries, conflicting, and unhealthy. On a good day, we'd have long car talks about random topics and exchange gifts on Valentine's Day. But pain still lingered in my heart, so we never got along for too long. When we weren't caught up in temporary lust, I was lashing out at him. Behind the persona, I wanted my life with my man back, to be happy and feel loved again. Zion was the closest thing to it.

He changed and was no longer the person I had fallen in love with. He was a new father, somebody else's man, caught in a lifestyle that no longer included our goals and dreams or protecting me. Zion wanted me to remain the same girl from our relationship without considering how this situation had affected me. He figured maintaining contact with me and saying that he didn't want to lose me and he loved me was enough to ease my pain and sweep our problems away. But love is an action, and his actions reminded me of my parents' actions—careless and selfish. He claimed to not want to lose me but in the same sentence would explain that he wanted to be a good father, which included being in a relationship with the mother of his child. The idea stemmed from his own childhood experience, which is his details to share. I still don't know how he made sense of it, but if you asked him today, he'd deny it.

The situation was a mess and wasn't working for me. I wanted Zion to leave me alone. We'd stop communicating for a few months, but that didn't last either. I'd get a random call at 6 a.m. or an e-mail asking for help with his school schedule, or he'd use his favorite line: "I need to talk to you." And like that, I'd give in, our roller-coaster love continued.

The hardest part was that I didn't want to hate him. I didn't want to be consumed with anger and bitterness from hating yet another person. But I was twenty-one years old in a self-made unhealthy situation, only hurting myself by trying to hold on to what was. I had tried marijuana before and didn't like it. I matched discomfort with the heavy use of alcohol, turning to liquor when my nerves were riled up. I would end what was supposed to be a casual night out with friends by exposing my deepest emotions with lack of self-control, shouting, and crying about how I felt about losing Zion and his deceitful ways, criticizing the happy life he portrayed on Instagram. The next morning, I would be disappointed in myself, regretting the way I had acted. If I was with Zion, sometimes I'd lash out and fight him. I was a different person under the influence. I found that the worst part of drinking liquor was the decline from being wasted to sobriety. My emotions poured uncontrollably out of my heart with a heavy and stingy feeling. I had two choices: drown myself in alcohol to remain numb or don't drink at all to maintain self-control. I didn't want to be an alcoholic. I didn't want to continue the vicious cycle of substance abuse attacking my family. I didn't like the drunk me. I knew I was better than that. I continued to drink while repeatedly promising that I would stop, and I gradually put the cup down.

Even after the whole fiasco, Zion and I decided to give our relationship another try. I never stopped loving him. I still believed in us. He would say, "Kenisha, be optimistic." I couldn't see myself in a relationship with anyone else, and the possessive woman in me didn't want to see him with anyone else. Zion still can't give me a valid reason for his actions. He'll talk in circles, blabber that he felt unneeded in the relationship, remind me that I said no when he asked me to bear his child and sum it up to being a lost boy at the time. My upbringing had instilled fear into me. I was scared to become a mother because I'd seen how easy it was for my parents to walk away from me. I did not want to be put in a position to do the same to my own child. Even with knowing myself and knowing I could never stomach abandoning my child, the thought of having a child gave me anxiety. My childhood caused me not to depend on others. I'd rather do things myself to avoid disappointment. And I didn't want to be like my mom when it came to men—dependent and hopeless. But it was something I was willing to work on for him.

I'd never seen a healthy blended family. All I had witnessed was baby mama and girlfriend drama. It seems that most people I know think it's abnormal for the two to get along, which isn't true. And, for sure, I didn't want a negative experience like the ones I had seen. I had no interest in arguing or fighting with a woman for no profound reason. And I had no desire to be with a man who didn't have a healthy relationship with the mother of his child. To educate myself, I listened to Jada Pinkett-Smith, her daughter, Willow, and her mother, Adrienne, discuss the topic on Red Table Talk. I aspire to be mature like Jada, allowing Will Smith and the mother of his child to travel with their son to experience his parents together in a positive light. I also watched Swizz Beats' ex-wife Mashonda's interview about her struggles with his infidelity and having a positive working blended family. For her, establishing a relationship with Alicia Keys outside of her son and his father worked. Once Mashonda got to know Alicia, the relationship flourished. Both women's experiences showed that the process of becoming a healthy blended family could be challenging.

Zion listened on his own time as well. Together, we discussed what we learned and how we'd apply it to our lives. Our conversations explored our comfort levels, likes, and dislikes. If a vacation was planned, we would all go. The activities would be kid friendly, and no one would be allowed to drift off to leave the others to be babysitters.

But our attempt to replicate what we had learned led to dysfunction between him, the mother of his child, his sister, and me. His sister was once my dearest friend. She was one of the few people I'd communicated with when Zion and I weren't together. We'd text all day. Our conversations were filled with jokes and laughter. We maintained a tight bond that was ruined by her desire for Zion and me to have a relationship without his son. Of course, I didn't agree. I didn't understand how a healthy relationship could be possible under those conditions. How could we move forward if we didn't embrace the new dynamics of our relationship and address the underlying issues? And how could we be happy living by the ideals of someone who wasn't a factor in the relationship? The only people that mattered were Zion, the mother of his child, his son and me.

I still can't identify the problem. I was in the middle of something that I can't quite put my finger on, and when Zion became incarcerated, I was left to figure things out on my own. His sister claimed the child's mother didn't like me. And if she found out I was around her son, she'd take him away. However, during a four-hour one-on-one conversation with the child's mother, she denied it, claiming she'd never said such a thing. She said she didn't have an issue with me and never threatened to keep her son away for any reason. She admitted that she wasn't ready for me to be one on one with her son, which I respected.

As Jada and Mashonda had expressed, the process takes time. By the end of our conversation, we agreed that if there were any future issues, we'd contact each other to resolve them. I thought that after an in-depth conversation, clearing the air, understanding each other's perspectives, and sharing our insecurities, we were a step closer to having a healthy, blended family. Wishful thinking.

It wasn't long before I reached my breaking point due to yet another incident. His sister called me yelling about several things, reminding me that I wasn't a mother, accusing me of taking pictures with the child. Pictures that never existed. She accused me of telling the child I was his step-mom because I was in a relationship with his father. What could I have gained from telling a four-year-old that? Absolutely nothing. Again, she repeated that his mother didn't want me around him. I rebutted her argument, denying the accusations and informing her that his mother and I had spoken and had an understanding. If there was an issue, she could contact me. Unfortunately, she didn't want to hear the truth and continued her rant.

We were friends, so, to me, the situation wasn't worth arguing about. I tried to get to the root of the issue and asked her for the source of the rumors. She claimed that one of her and Zion's sisters had said it. With the phone on speaker, I confronted the only sister that was in the house with the child and me that morning. She denied telling her any of it, so I was confused and frustrated. It didn't make sense. Why would my friend make up a lie? Why would she not want to see my relationship restored and thriving? Not only was I disturbed by the negative effects this was having on my relationship, but I was losing my friends at the same time.

As agreed, I tried giving the child's mother a call to cease the chaos. I figured if she let everyone know that we didn't have an issue, the problem would go away. And afterward, if anyone continued with any foolishness, it would be clear that they were the problem. She didn't answer or return my calls or text messages.

Later that evening, Zion called me from jail. I spoke with him, letting him know what had occurred earlier that day. He tended to take a neutral stance as if he was skeptical about how I may have contributed to the problem. His response was not that of a man with whom I desired to have a healthy blended family. He never acknowledged that his family was wrong, and he showed no interest in bringing the truth to light.

Zion said, "If I go against my family, and you leave, then I won't have anybody." Although he reiterated that he loved me and wanted to be with me and advised me to not worry about it, his response left me in a different head space. He felt there was nothing he could do about the situation since he was incarcerated. He didn't understand that I was the one being attacked, and, unfortunately, it wasn't something I was interested in putting off because of how sensitive I was about the topic. And there was no valid basis to the problem in my eyes. At least he could've defended me and checked his sister.

I was even more upset with Zion. I blamed him. I was experiencing this chaos because of his infidelity. I hadn't fallen in love with a man who had a child. I didn't ask for any of this. I also blamed him for allowing the situation to go on for so long and felt he contributed to the dysfunction. It was like he couldn't put himself in my shoes and see things from my perspective or be a man. I was the one dealing with the headaches and stress. He was aware of the precautions I'd taken to eliminate problems.

I distanced myself from his child, but that upset him. It made him feel like I didn't accept his child, as he had claimed on several instances. But when I at least said hi to his son, it caused other problems. I couldn't win for losing.

In the end, things were weird and didn't make a bit of sense to me. I couldn't decipher the truth from a lie. Was my friend acting this way because she was defending the mother's wishes and her relationship with her nephew? Or did she have some other issue against me—was she using this situation as a smokescreen? Either way, I wasn't doing any of the things she had accused me of. I wasn't going to allow people to play on my emotional scars, so I decided it was best I separate myself. I cut ties with my friends, and although, out of anger, I'd expressed to Zion that I no longer wanted to be in the relationship, we didn't break up.

The situation reminded me that people will always put their family first.

I was mentally and emotionally exhausted, overwhelmed by thoughts about the root causes of the problem—his cheating and my abandonment issues. Sounding like a crazy woman, I imposed boundaries on our relationship to protect my peace, causing more problems between Zion and me. I let him know I didn't want his family anywhere near me. They weren't welcome in our house. I would not be in attendance for any family events. They no longer existed to me, and I didn't want to hear anything about any of them. I prohibited my future children from meeting his family, and, finally, I declared that his son was non-existent in my world and our relationship. I washed my hands of the situation with no desire to revisit it in the future.

I was compromising with myself, pretending I didn't value family and friendship and redefining my definition of a union with a man. I questioned why I allowed myself to stay in the relationship for so long. I was unsure if I wanted to continue the relationship, because it reminded me that there was an important part of my boyfriend I couldn't be a part of. I was driving myself crazy because I knew I didn't want to be that kind of person or have that kind of life. I had dealt with dysfunctional relationships as a child and refused to continue the pattern as an adult. At no fault of my own, I was excluded and could no longer be involved with people I once considered my family. My feelings and wants were ignored in a situation that had everything to do with my life. I felt abandoned again. I realized my pain was deeper; it was my childhood trauma resurfacing.

After avoiding therapeutic treatment for many years, I decided to give therapy a chance, especially after recommending it to everyone else. At age twenty-seven, I was a bubble filled with tears as I walked into my first therapy session. My therapist asked me one question, and the moment I began talking, I started crying. I was all over the place as I educated my therapist about my life experiences, starting from my childhood. In no specific order, I let it all out, exceeding our one-hour session.

As we continued sessions, we unpacked everything I had told her. The first lesson I learned was that I can't control the actions of others, and their actions have nothing to do with me. I realized everything that had a good outcome in my life had structure, like school. If I studied and completed the assignments, I'd pass. But that's not how life goes. Even if I have good intentions and I am my best self with people, it's up to them to return the same energy. But no matter what actions they choose, it has nothing to do with me. It doesn't define who I am or my worth. Ultimately, I learned to respond to these situations like Angela Davis: "I am no longer accepting the things I cannot change; I am changing the things I cannot accept."

I was on a wild goose chase looking for family, love, and belonging outside of those who had hurt me. It dawned on me to reevaluate my idea of family. I thought of Ashley. I realized that although we had yet to discuss my sexual assault, over the years, we had managed to rebuild our sisterly bond through actions. We've lived together again, supported each other, and shared our first glass of wine. I believe my sister has her own trauma because of what happened to us. As a person who understands the effects of trauma, I've forgiven her. She is my family.

It has only been a few months since I've started this journey. I attend therapy once a week, and I am learning more about what triggers my anxiety, new coping skills, how to communicate without shutting down, and letting go of unhealthy habits and relationships. I'm doing the work in individual therapy to confront my past, work on myself, and process everything I have been suppressing.

Allow Me to Reintroduce Myself

"My mission in life is not to survive, but to thrive; and to do so with some passion, some compassion, some humor and some style."
- **Dr. Maya Angelou**

I'd heard the theory of Maslow's Hierarchy of Needs a hundred times before I grasped its concept. It wasn't until my second semester at Florida State University, when a social work professor reintroduced the philosophy, that I understood it.

In the linear notes of the Hierarchy of Needs, Abraham Maslow emphasized: "The urge of self-actualization is rooted in the human psyche but only surfaces once basic needs are fulfilled." Once a person fulfills the need for food, security, love, and self-esteem, he/she finds a desire for creative expression that ultimately allows self-actualization to arise. To understand human motivation and the pursuit of happiness, he created a list of basic human needs to be fulfilled to reach the highest level of psychological health: physiological, safety, love/belonging, esteem, and self-actualization.

For so long, I was in search of finding where I belonged, feeling like a ping-pong ball longing for basic things like a safe home, security, love, acceptance, and to be treated with dignity. I nearly lost myself along the way. Life showed me rough times, and I spent a great deal of those times feeling unfortunate and surviving every emotion, realizing that yearning for love from others was a waste of my time. I'd lost count of how many chances I'd given people to love me, and disappointed myself in the process. I could no longer blame them for situations I'd brought upon myself. I understood that sometimes, we're better off without what we think we need to reach self-actualization. It took me more than enough time to reach this level of consciousness, realizing that I was allowing the burdens of resentment, disappointment, and doubt to drive my life, unaware that people's actions don't define who I am or who I'd grow up to be. I stare at my reflection in the mirror, wondering how I ever contemplated suicide. I'm worthy, and now I know the beauty in that.

Growing up without positive role models in environments that easily influenced my behavior almost ruined me. I was a product of my environment and mesmerized by material things, other's lives, their blessings, relationships, style, and beauty, making it easier for me to suffer from the hard knocks of the world. I had nobody to tell me right from wrong, so I normalized struggle as the way of life. Some like to say I've been here before because, early on, I realized the way we were living wasn't all life had to offer. Nobody I knew had made it to be like anyone I'd seen on television. Nobody was happy. I could feel the negative, dark, heavy energy all around me. All of us lusting over things we didn't have. But I knew there was more to life than what I had known life to be.

I steadily ask myself in amazement, "How did I make it out?" Others ask what changed me. To try to find the answer, I had to go back to my roots. It was the gems that Mr. Rogers had planted into my psyche. I don't remember the last time I've seen an episode of the show, but I remember Mr. Rogers' sweater, the trolley, and his voice. He said, "Look for helpers." So, during my distress, I looked for helpers. I watched television series like *The Cosby Show, Diff'rent Strokes, What's Happening?, Good Times, A Different World, The Fresh Prince of Bel-Air, Moesha*, and all the other black 90s sitcoms. At different parts of my life, I aligned myself with some of the shows' characters, such as Arnold Jackson, Kimberly Reese, Whitley, Dwayne, Lena James, Will, and Dorian. The shows influenced me, planting learnable lessons, and represented everything I believe in—the importance of being proud to be black, self-love, education, family, friends, growth, and a sense of purpose.

...

There's a saying that when a woman cuts her hair, she is about to change her life. In the safe space of my student housing apartment, feeling like a caterpillar anxious to evolve into a butterfly, I underwent the big chop, getting rid of processed hair and split ends. I had broken out of my cocoon and was ready to live a new life as a self-defined woman.

When asked who Kenisha is, I respond with immediate thoughts from system one of my mind, an automatic and fast kind of thinking that requires little energy and attention. I mention my struggle, highlighting what I've been through, never disregarding that my struggle has defined some prominent moments on my journey. My struggle has given me something to be proud of. It has provided me with the expertise to be relatable and prosper in pursuit of my passion and understand who I am. But it doesn't define all of me.

Afforded the opportunity to reap the benefits of feeling free and seeing things through a clear lens, I no longer suffer from the sorrows of struggle, but I flourish in the beauty of overcoming. I am a student of life and my own experiences. I'm in control, and I set the rules, morals, and standards by which I choose to live by. And now I want to know myself beyond the struggle and accolades. I'm at a place in life where my brain is not occupied by strategizing to survive and make a way for myself. So far, I know that I appreciate the simple things in life like a stroll through nature, a day at the beach, a good book, and a fresh acai bowl from Raw Juce, my favorite juice bar. I realize the best things in life are free—happiness and peace. And neither are worth sacrificing. I've created a bucket list of all the things I want to do, and I check them off as I go.

I'm busy learning to become who my soul knows. My authentic life is just beginning. I don't know what more it has in store for me, but I'm ready for whatever's to come. Just as my hair grows in its natural state, I'll get to know Kenisha from the natural state of her heart and soul, so I can tell you who she is later. Like Nipsey Hussle said, "Life is not a sprint, it's a marathon, and the marathon does continue."

You are not your circumstances.

Younger

Challenge

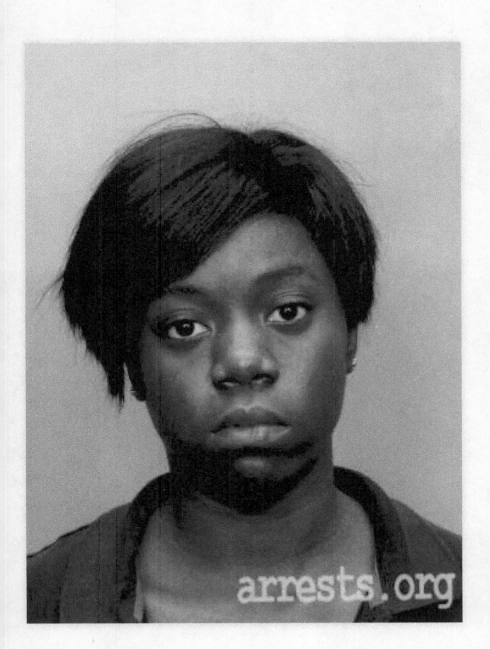

Educated

SOMETHING TO LEARN ABOUT: The Affordable Care Act gives former foster kids like Miami Dade College right with her younger sister Mylika, healthcare benefits to age 26, though they may not know it.

Congresswoman
FREDERICA S. WILSON
Congratulates the recipients of the
Florida Congressional District 24
2014 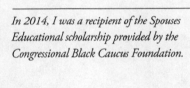 Congressional Black Caucus **FOUNDATION** Scholarship

Kenisha Anthony
Florida State
University

Batche Fils-Aime
Nova Southeastern
University

Chazre Hill
Florida A&M
University

Carl Hughes
University of
Central Florida

Myles Johnson
Florida A&M
University

Asim Lynch
Florida International
University

Rashad Revere
Clark Atlanta
University

Richie Revere
Clark Atlanta
University

L DIAZ/ MIAMI HERALD STAFF
sha Anthony, at

In 2014, I was a recipient of the Spouses
Educational scholarship provided by the
Congressional Black Caucus Foundation.

After my graduation ceremony, Mylika and I did a photo
op for an article in the Miami Herald. This day, I earned
my Associate of Arts degree.

I was reminded better was soon to come.

The celebration of earning a Bachelor of Social Work

Trust is gained when we break bread together.

The celebration of earning
a Master of Public Administration

Explorer

A day exploring the beauty of
Prague, Czech Republic

Here I am at the wall dedicated to the memory of the late John Lennon

Cesky Krumlov

I do not like chocolate.
My s'mores cake was only crackers
and marshmallow.

I did good for my first time.

Here I am at the Eiffel Tower

————————

Passion

FLORIDA STATE UNIVERSITY
College of Social Work

csw.fsu.ed

Change a life. **Start** with yours.

Change a life,
start with yours

Florida Children's First presented me the Youth Advocate of the Year award

I was hoping to see the Obamas
my first time in the White House

Growing

You are your possibilities.

Know Your Rights

CHILDREN IN FOSTER CARE HAVE THE RIGHT[1]:

To NOT remain silent.

To live in a safe, healthful, and comfortable home where he or she is treated with respect and provided with healthful food, appropriate clothing, and adequate storage space for personal use and where the caregiver is aware of and understands the child's history, needs, and risk factors and respects the child's preferences for attending religious services and activities.

To be free from physical, sexual, emotional, or other abuse, or corporal punishment.

To receive medical, dental, vision, and mental health services, as needed.

To be able to have contact and visitation with his or her parents, other family members, and fictive kin and to be placed with his or her siblings and, if not placed together with his or her siblings, to have frequent visitation and ongoing contact with his or her siblings.

To be able to contact the Florida Children's Ombudsman, as described in s. 39.4088, regarding violations of rights; to speak to the ombudsman

---

1   A Bill of Rights does not exist in the State of Florida. This legislative session Florida Youth Shine will be advocating for youth in foster care to have a Foster Care Bill of Rights. Contact your local legislator to gain their support in the passing of SB 496.

confidentially; and to be free from threats or punishment for making complaints.

Heather Rosenberg
Direct: (850)717-4505
Cell: (850)491-2203
E-Mail: kidsfla@myflfamilies.com
(844)KIDS-FLA

To attend school and participate in extracurricular, cultural, and personal enrichment activities.

To attend independent living program classes and activities.

To attend all court hearings and address the court.

To have fair and equal access to all available services, placement, care, treatment, and benefits.

To have access to existing information regarding the educational and financial assistance options available to him or her.

To have a guardian ad litem appointed to represent his or her best interests and, if appropriate, an attorney appointed to represent his or her legal interests.

Playlist

This playlist of music has been the background of my life throughout this journey of writing, reflecting, and growing.

Title: *A Memoir*
Available on Spotify, Apple Music and Tidal

DREAMS | SOLANGE

BAD IDEA | YBN CORDAE

RUNAWAY LOVE | LUDACRIS

GETAWAY | MONICA

THIS TOO SHALL PASS | INDIA ARIE

STAY WOKE | MEEK MILL

CHANGES | TUPAC SHAKUR

PEDESTALS | SOLANGE

DEAR MAMA | TUPAC SHAKUR

FUCK OFF | TEIRRA WHACK

MISEDUCATION OF LAURYN HILL | LAURYN HILL

STRENGTH, COURAGE & WISDOM | INDIA ARIE

INTRO | J. COLE

CRANES IN THE SKY | SOLANGE

LOVE YOURZ | J. COLE

PEOPLE MAKE THE WORLD GO ROUND | THE STYLISTICS

DON'T TOUCH MY HAIR | SOLANGE

BROWN SKIN GIRL | BEYONCE

IMAN | RAPSODY

HIGH RISES | CHIKA

REAL BIG | NIPSEY HUSSLE

LOVE | MUSIQ SOULCHILD

A CHANGE IS GONNA COME | SAM COOKE

LAILA'S WISDOM | RAPSODY

LOVE TO THE PEOPLE | CURTIS MAYFIELD

GLOSSARY[1]

Adoption Home Study – a screening of the home and life of prospective adoptive parents prior to allowing an adoption to take place.

Aged Out – a term used to refer to a child within a state's foster care system who is still in the system when they reach age 18.

Another Planned Permanent Living Arrangement (APPLA) – the least preferred permanency option, "planned" means the arrangement is intended, designed, considered or deliberate. "Permanent" means enduring, lasting, or stable. The term "living arrangement" includes not only the physical placement of the child or young adult, but also quality of care, stability, supervision, and nurturing a youth will receive.

Bio-Parent Visit - a meeting to discuss the status of the case and progress in services and assess for further needs with biological parents. It must be completed every twenty-five days and required by law.

Case Plan - the department shall prepare a draft document for each child receiving services. A detailed description and logistics of each service should be included. Parents must participate in the process. This document must be approved by the courts.

Child Resource Record (CRR) previously known as "Bluebook" – a standardized record developed and maintained for every child entering out-of-home care that contains copies of the basic legal, demographic, educational,

1   **Source** — Child Welfare Information Gateway https://www.childwelfare.gov/pubPDFs/cw_educators.pdf

medical, and psychological information pertaining to a specific child.

Child Welfare – an umbrella term that refers to a spectrum of services offered by child welfare agencies designed to protect the welfare of children and provide families with the support to properly care for their children.

Dependency Case – a case brought before the Court based on allegations of abuse, abandonment, and neglect of a child. The term "dependency" is based on the idea of a child being dependent on the State or Court to provide help and services.

Foster Child – a child raised by someone who is not its natural or adoptive parent.

Foster Parent – a person who cares for children who have entered the foster care system.

In-home Assessment - an evaluation of the home and life of parents whose children will remain in their care during a dependency case.

Judicial Review - (a) the court shall have continuing jurisdiction in accordance with this section and shall review the status of the child's well-being and case at least every six months as required by this subsection or more frequently if the court deems it necessary or desirable.

Normalcy – the act of participating in "normal life" activities.

Permanency - having positive, healthy, nurturing relationships with adults who provide emotional, financial, moral, educational, and other kinds of support as youth mature into adults.

Respite Care – a "short-term" foster placement used when one foster family temporarily cares for another family's foster child.

Reunification – a permanency option, it is a process to return a child to the custody of his/her parent, getting a family safely back together.

Safety Plan – a personalized, practical plan that can help you avoid dangerous situations and know the best way to react when you are in danger.

Terminated Parental Rights (TPR'd) – the legal termination of a mother or father as the parent of a child.

ACKNOWLEDGEMENTS

No one ever said it would be easy, but I made it through. I'll start by first thanking myself. Thank you, Kenisha, for being patient with yourself, dedicated, resilient, and selfless. I'd like to thank God for His grace and blessings.

A person who becomes self-sufficient by overcoming hurdles due to lack of support by the child welfare system is not a success story for the system. When all failed, my community stayed strong! I am the product of your dedication to service. I am blessed to have had your support and continued mentorship on this journey:

A special thank you to

Florida's Children First, Florida Youth Shine
Advocacy, Mentorship

Emy's Promise
Educational Scholarship, Mentorship, Forever Family

Florida Foster Care Review
Career, Mentorship

Foster Club
Advocacy

Foster Shock, Mari Frankel
Advocacy

International Student Foundation
Educational Scholarship

Congressional Black Caucus Foundation, Congresswoman Frederica Wilson
Educational Scholarship

Miami Foundation, Miami-Dade County Public School
Educational Scholarship

Gilman International Program
Study Abroad Scholarship

Miami Dade College - TRIO, Single Stop, and ICED
Education, Mentorship

Florida State University - College of Social Work, Unconquered Scholars
Education, Scholarship, Foster Care Liaison Program

Florida International University - Fostering Panther Pride
Education, Foster Care Liaison Program

National Foster Youth Institute
Advocacy